MW00718058

Offshoring Secrets

Building and Running a Successful
India Operation

By Utkarsh Rai

20660 Stevens Creek Blvd.
Suite 210
Cupertino, CA 95014

First Printing: September, 2007
Paperback ISBN: 1600050611 (978-1-60005-061-9)
Place of Publication: Silicon Valley, California, USA
Paperback Library of Congress Number: 2007935613

eBook ISBN: 160005062X (978-1-60005-062-6)

Trademarks

Warning and Disclaimer

Endorsements of "Offshoring Secrets"

"While many have read about outsourcing in India and China, Utkarsh truly 'owns' the experience of establishing multiple, successful, operations in India and speaks from both his mind and his heart in this book. Utkarsh is a wise advisor when he creates case studies to put you in the other person's shoes to understand the environment that person or work group lives in."
Mr. Gary Rieschel, Founder and Managing Director, Qiming Venture Partners, China

"Utkarsh's book, drawn from his substantial experience in working in this industry and then steering a start-up to success. This is an excellent primer not only for those intending to start operations in the already overheated IT industry in India, but also for those who are already running operations and are facing numerous challenges to be successful."
Mr. Sammy Sana, Managing Director, Motorola Software Group, India Design Center

"While guarding a reader on the likely pitfalls on the way, the author systematically takes a reader through all aspects of implementation; be it hiring an office space, recruiting staff, or managing cultural differences. How to manage expectations of the parent company while simultaneously addressing local issues have been dealt with in great detail."
Mr. Ravi Sangal, Former President, International Data Corporation (IDC) India Ltd, President (Corporate), Cyber Media India Ltd

"Utkarsh has experienced off-shoring himself, that is evident from the way he writes this book. From that experience, he provides a full spectrum of all the important aspects of an off-shoring operation, in great practical detail."
Dr. Bob Hoekstra, Opportunity India Management Consulting, Holland and former CEO Philips Innovation Campus, India

Acknowledgements

Many people have contributed in making this book a reality:

First and foremost, Deepti, my wife, who supported me from start to finish, without her, this book would not be feasible.

Ashok Samalam, who has been a helpful critique, which helped in improving the flow of this book.

Steven Hand, who has patiently reviewed the book and provided invaluable comments.

Sudhanshu Verma and Parthiban Kandappan, for providing the feedback on specific chapters.

Dan Benas and Tapan Mohanti have validated some of the points from this book with their own experiences in working with India.

Jagdeep Singh, Drew Perkins, Dave Welch, Tom Fallon, Rusty Cumpston and Paul Whitney for providing overall support.

Rajesh Setty for helping me through every step in getting this book published.

Karthik Sundaram, not only for editing this book, but also for providing an outsider perspective.

Mitchell Levy, my publisher, who mastered the art of multi-tasking and quick decision making, helped in bringing out this book at the earliest.

Vinod Khosla for writing the foreword of this book, which served as a great morale booster.

Gary Rieschel, Bob Hoekstra, Sammy Sana and Ravi Sangal, residing in different geographies and gurus in their respective fields, have written some beautiful comments.

The acknowledgement will be incomplete without the mention of my mother and mentor Indira, father Upendra, brother Harsh, sister Anshu and brother-in-law Alok.

Last but not the least, my colleagues in Infinera and former colleagues in Siemens, Adaptec and Motorola for providing me valuable experiences in writing this book.

Dedication

Utsav, my son and Vidushi, my daughter, for allowing me to steal some of their share of my time to write this book.

A Message From Happy About®

Thank you for your purchase of this Happy About book. It is available online at http://happyabout.info/offshoring-secrets.php or at other online and physical bookstores.

- Please contact us for quantity discounts at sales@happyabout.info
- If you want to be informed by e-mail of upcoming Happy About® books, please e-mail bookupdate@happyabout.info

Happy About is interested in you if you are an author who would like to submit a non-fiction book proposal or a corporation that would like to have a book written for you. Please contact us by e-mail editorial@happyabout.info or phone (1-408-257-3000).

Other Happy About books available include:

- The Home Run Hitter's Guide to Fundraising
  http://happyabout.info/homerun-fundraising.php
- Overcoming Inventoritis:
  http://happyabout.info/overcoming-inventoritis.php
- Tales From the Networking Community
  http://happyabout.info/networking-community.php
- Happy About Online Networking:
  http://happyabout.info/onlinenetworking.php
- Happy About LinkedIn for Recruiting:
  http://happyabout.info/linkedin4recruiting.php
- Climbing the Ladder of Business Intelligence
  http://happyabout.info/climbing-ladder.php
- The Business Rule Revolution:
  http://happyabout.info/business-rule-revolution.php
- Happy About Global Software Test Automation:
  http://www.happyabout.info/globalswtestautomation.php
- Happy About Joint Venturing:
  http://happyabout.info/jointventuring.php

Contents

Foreword by Vinod Khosla

The 21st century has witnessed a spurt in the growth of many organizations that chose to open their own India operations in the hopes of having better control on the quality of the products and people, intellectual property and execution of various state-of-the-art projects. Today, managers face extreme adjustments as each local economy transforms into a global economy, which in turn, causes changes to the work environment. The most significant issue facing offshore organizations as global competition increases is the concept of sustaining a successful operation.

Plenty of articles explain outsourcing and its impact on the global economy, but very few tackle the challenges of offshoring. Utkarsh Rai recognized the common problems behind running a successful India operation. I have not come across any other book, wherein a true insider writes about "HOW" to build and administer a successful operation.

This book outlines the environmental changes within an offshore organization and its management consequences. Offshoring is increasing dramatically in India, but a company wishing to setup an office or delegate a project to an India offshore organization should understand and anticipate potential management issues. The management needs to set up a practical and logical framework to understand offshoring – Utkarsh explains just that.

I have seen organizations that have struggled to survive, took time in becoming productive, have been unable to breakeven in the stipulated timeframe, or have had a difficult time to inculcate the same culture in the new setup and experienced other issues, which are all equally responsible in hindering the growth of India offshore center.

This book is an exceptional mix of offshoring theories and practices, helping companies understand the reasons for what management in both the parent company and offshore counterparts are facing today. If the management from both parties were to be better educated on the perception of India offshoring, any company can succeed in running an offshore entity.

This book not only provides many insights, but also contains an excellent set of case studies, which companies and individuals currently experience in day-to-day operations and provides possible, yet provoking, points to solve them. Utkarsh provides a clear understanding of offshoring developments, offering new approaches for management to achieve more flexibility and greater efficiency, which in turn, provides greater cost-effectiveness.

I have interacted with Utkarsh on multiple occasions. I am convinced that his experience and concept of offshore management will help many companies and individuals – both setting up a new offshore center, or those already running an offshore organization – to learn and apply relevant management practices that could ensure successful operations daily.

As a venture capitalist, I will be the first to recommend this book to my portfolio companies, even as we look for economizing our operations.

Each chapter of this book could stand on its own, but the flow of theory and logic results in a practical appreciation of the issues we face in the India offshore center. Enjoy this reading, and, hopefully, you can apply the management practices and theories Utkarsh has written for the success of your own business enterprise.

Vinod Khosla

Preface for "Offshoring Secrets"

If you have picked up this book or are thinking of purchasing it, you are most likely a manager of an Indian operation with a global company. On the other hand, maybe you are the executive with the parent company, in charge of the India operations. Or perhaps you are simply exploring offshore opportunities. Regardless of your position, this book answers many questions faced by individuals who have a vested interest in India offshore centers. Questions such as:

- My manager has asked me to setup an India center to save costs, but I am not achieving any remarkable savings within the stipulated timeframe. What am I doing wrong?

- Why am I always surprised at the results when the end of an execution cycle is nearing?

- We provide a very competitive salary review every year but why is our attrition still so high?

- Why am I unable to foresee people issues in India and unable to manage these issues efficiently and effectively?

- I am tired of traveling to India to put out one fire after another. Why do these issues seem commonplace in India, but never seem to be a problem with our parent company?

- How can I say no to a new change request to the parent company, as this will affect the schedule?

- How do I allay fears within the parent company about two employees in India who freely discuss their salaries or positions within the company?

- I am frustrated that even after I foresaw and raised the risk three months ago, the overseas manager is now asking for a reason.

- The parent company does not realize the turmoil in the Indian employment market, and has set ambitious recruiting plans. How do I make them work in accord with the state of the market here?

Although India is a great destination for an offshore experiment to reduce costs, improved efficiency and a shortened time-to-market, delivering a seamless offshore experience is not easy and is not a fully stable process. Unrealistic expectations, hidden pitfalls, unexpected twists in policies, markets, and strategies can create hurdles that can disrupt even the simplest of an offshore exercise.

When I started my career in the late eighties, my colleagues and I were one of the first few batches of IT professionals who joined Siemens in India and went on to work, with Siemens Germany. We returned to form a spin-off called Siemens Information Systems in India, an IT company.

I moved on to work with Adaptec in the Silicon Valley, where I was involved in a full-blown product development lifecycle. In the boom period of the late nineties, when Indians flooded the U.S. in search of IT jobs, it became clear that India—Bangalore, specifically—could be a thriving center for product development. I flew against the blowing winds and joined the Global Software Group at Motorola in Bangalore.

This opportunity provided an abundance of experience in leading large teams, recruiting a large pool of engineers and handling complex people issues. When the first Motorola facilities in Bangalore were filling up, we moved to a new location elsewhere in the city, and that provided me an even greater framework about challenges involving a new setup. As I grew to become a member of the senior management team of Motorola in Bangalore, I handled operational issues like crisis management, adherence to government regulations and execution challenges.

All of my previous experiences prepared me for my current role as the head of India operations for Infinera—a startup in digital optical networking (which went IPO in June 2007)—a position that I took up in early 2003. At that time, when only a few people were on board, I was responsible for reinforcing the company culture and its policies, ramping up the team in number and in skills. My experiences have helped us achieve a smooth execution with ownership and a steady and progressive drive from India. We have understood the Indian Government's regulations and operational compliance, and have setup a new facility in line with our expansion plan. However, our biggest success has been in managing and developing a company's greatest asset—its people.

This book is an in-depth analysis of my own experiences and interactions with various people in the industry. This book is written for both Indian and overseas audiences, who are involved in setting up the operation, executing projects and working in support organization like the HR, Administration, and Finance.

The ninth Annual Global CEO survey by PricewaterhouseCoopers stated that 44% of the CEOs interviewed are planning to open up an office in India[1]. If you are one of the 44% or are thinking of raising the percentage, then this book can help lay the blueprint for success.

It is unfair to pinpoint any one factor as responsible for the success of our India office, but if asked to choose one, I would have to state the "passion to make it successful" is what has helped us succeed. Therefore, it is you—and only you—who can make it happen. So grab the opportunity and make it happen.

Utkarsh Rai
Bangalore, India

---

1. 9th Annual Global CEO Survey, Globalisation and Complexity, Inevitable Forces in a Changing Economy, PriceWaterHouseCoopers

1 A Brief History

India has always played a major role in the world's economy since the beginning of written history. A strong influence in the Indo-China region, more familiarly known as East Asia, Indian rulers have led numerous expeditions and have given spread to religions such as Hinduism and Buddhism. With a robust agrarian community that supported monarchy rule, India grew mightily in population. This abundance of talent allowed the then-ruling British Empire to send people off as indentured laborers to far off places such as Mauritius, South Africa, Surinam, Guiana, the West Indies and Fiji in order to help boost these countries' economies. Indian businesspersons and skilled laborers traveled and settled in those countries as well as other countries of the African continent, while the spread of tea plantations triggered migration to Myanmar, Sri Lanka, Malaysia and Singapore during this same period.

When India gained its independence in 1947, Europe—mainly Britain—was received with a sizeable number of Indian immigrants. During the cold war era, the Eastern block countries came in closer contact with India through economic and political cooperation—marked by India's famous Non-Aligned Movement. The oil boom in the seventies led to the increase of India's presence in the Gulf. Slowly, Australia, Canada, New Zealand and many other countries experienced an increase in Indian settlements as well. Currently, over 25 million people of Indian origin are living outside of India and are actively contributing to the world economy[2].

Through the constant emigration of its people's, the Indian economy itself did not really take off until the Nineteen Eighties, despite a young population of over one billion. Although the mid-seventies introduced computer science as a college curriculum, the importance of this science only became evident much later. This relatively new science was the cornerstone of the revival of the Indian economy, which had been plodding along after centuries of British rule. Only in the middle of the last century had the United States opened up immigration for Indians. The subsequent growth of the information technology industry in the United States propelled the growth of the Indian. Many migrants came to the U.S. seeking a higher education and settled down with jobs in the IT industry. Back in India, Wipro, TCS and HCL were leading the way, where Infosys had just formed and was at a nascent stage. The government institutions themselves were the torchbearers of high quality work—Uptron, Keltron, CMC, NIC, C-DOT and so on. The city of Bangalore attracted very high quality talents that took charge in developing government defense projects.

This was the time when the Internet age and faster communications catalyzed globalization. With the economy starting to open up, it triggered the first wave of India development centers, lead by companies such as Texas Instruments, which set up operations in Bangalore. People from both the existing IT workforce and from the government labs and institutions met their organizational requirements.

By this time, engineering colleges in India were offering computer science as a full four-year program. Many of the first graduates went abroad for higher studies and settled down in their country of education—predominantly in the U.S. Those who stayed behind also began to venture to different countries on specific assignments and mostly through their service companies. The "Y2K" fear played a key role in employing a major work force of immigrants in different

---

2. http://en.wikipedia.org/wiki/NRI

countries. This was the time when people from other engineering and sometimes pure science streams joined the IT bandwagon and went on overseas assignments. The National Institute of Information Technology (NIIT) had earned a reputation of providing excellent computer training to many ambitious immigrants. However, even well into the Nineties, most of the offshore Indian centers were not privy to more than a thousand employees.

With the economic downfall that befell the U.S. at the start of the new millennium, the once formidable IT industry came to a virtual standstill. The Indian IT industry experienced layoffs for the first time and salary hikes that people took for granted were frozen. In some cases, salary reductions became a consequence as well. However, those two years provided an opportunity for the next wave of IT in India.

The second wave of IT triggered many experienced Indians to start returning to India due to the economy meltdown in their country of residence. This reverse brain drain accelerated when governmental dictates in those countries, including cancellation of visas and reduction in the number of work permits, became pervasive. Organizations around the world struggled to return to profitability and looked to India with a fresh pair of eyes.

The biggest difference in the second wave of India's economic emergence was marked by the large influence of a new business entity: the emergence of pre-IPO startups in India. It has become a common phenomenon in the U.S. that new ventures will receive funding only if their business plan included an India or China strategy.

Thirty years ago, people held many reservations as to whether or not computer science was to be a viable career education, but the tide has turned. In addition to computer science, graduates from almost all disciplines of engineering and sometimes even pure science flock to IT and ITES industries. Indian companies employ more than 1.6 million people in IT and IT-enabled industries[3]. What makes the workforce even stronger is that many Indians are now fluent in English and have a proven track record to work easily amidst various cultures, providing international companies a unique destination to do business. The tighter intellectual property laws and the government's drive to set up

---

3. http://www.nasscom.in/Nasscom/templates/NormalPage.aspx?id=51851

software technology parks and export oriented units that gave quick approval to projects propelled the growth of interest. The growing economy of India—at an enviable 6% (or more) of GDP, and a vibrant democracy, provides a comfortable environment for investors.[4]

The IT sector has created history in India—not only in reviving the economy, but also by breaking from the past where multinationals either used India to market their product or migrate people from here to work at their locations. Today, India's established offshore centers achieve mission critical execution. According to a Software Technology Parks of India (STPI) report, four new companies pass the approval of licenses every week and the STPI units have been growing at CAGR of 13% in the last two years (2003-04 to 2005-06).[5]

This has also triggered many other sectors to open up to foreign investments, like biotechnology, insurance, automobiles, aeronautics, and pharmaceuticals. In addition, many multinational corporations have begun their own back office operations in India and some have collaborated with local companies for similar back-end processing. IT has also indirectly helped in the growth of other sectors (i.e. real estate, entertainment, travel, hospitality) by generating significant employment opportunities.

This unprecedented growth has set off many issues for companies and the industry. Hiring in big numbers has become the norm, and such a booming job market has made people choosy-work content and salary play a major factor in people's decision-making process. Attrition is rampant, even as accelerated hiring gives rise to competitive salary growth, leading to multiple job offers for a candidate. People have begun to simply shop without any motive to be hired, and "first day no show" has become a common and disappointing phenomenon. India, initially chosen for its low cost and high quality workforce, has started becoming a costly exercise. It has affected service companies greatly due to the predictable nature of their business and has forced them to seek new and innovative ways of reducing their costs. A junior engineer who drew a comparable salary of one sixth of that in the U.S. in the late nineties now draws around one fourth of the U.S. equivalent.

---

4. http://en.wikipedia.org/wiki/Economy_of_India
5. http://www.blr.stpi.in/

With high price tags, the expectation of output has also increased and the measure of success of an India center is based on many more parameters than it was in the last decade.

A Brief History Summarized:

It has not been as easy as one envisioned to set up or run an India center. Companies are discovering many strategic and tactical challenges. It requires strong leadership, a firm commitment to make the concept work, unambiguous and timely communication, excellent people skills, deep technical skills, a fine understanding of the Indian culture, and the right policies in place to be successful. However, the most important above all these factors is an environment of trust and the unwavering passion to be successful.

2 Choosing the Right Leader

Proper recruitment plays a critical role. Choosing the right person to lead is one of the most important decisions that a company has to make. Many factors play a role in deciding the ideal person to lead the team. Here are some of the most frequently discussed dilemmas:

- A strong technical person transferred from the parent company

- A strong technical person hired from the local market

- A strong general management person transferred from the parent company

- A strong general management person hired from the local market

- A strong sales/marketing person hired from the local market or transferred from the parent company

There are also many permutations and combinations to the situations mentioned above.

In a Fairly New Company

Start-ups setting up operations in India aim on making the setup functional as soon as possible and receiving deliverables as early as possible from a given entity. These startups normally have to choose between a strong technical person who can provide technical leadership and achieve the goal of providing fast deliverables or a general management person who is well versed in local issues like culture, government rules and regulations, hiring, retention, team building, compensation, and benefits.

People coming from the parent company to head the India operations face some common issues–an entirely different work culture and a newfound dynamism in the workforce. This directly influences building and retaining a team. A booming economy and an increasingly porous culture have brought changes in the social fabric, creating new and unique people issues.

Such a person will also struggle on the personal front. His family—also trying to settle down and adjust in India might decide to return home. The reasons may include problems with children adjusting to the school system, someone in the family unable to adjust to the climate and health issues, or the spouse may be dissatisfied with their job opportunities.

The head of the India operations has a twofold responsibility: the first is to setup the India office and the second, to build the team and ensure that they start making a valuable contribution as soon as possible. This can lead to frustration, as it can be difficult for them to do both functions within a given timeframe.

If he or she focuses on setting up the office, such a person will end up having almost no time for technical contribution. One solution is to require senior technical people from the parent office to visit for a few months and get the ball rolling.

If the head focuses on technical delivery, he will need to build the team with senior technical people that will contribute towards the product development. He will also have to work to increase the competency level of the team–and will need a strong support team to take care of various support functions like payroll, HR, and so on. While the India operations may choose to outsource some of the support, it will remain a challenge to manage the outsourcing to ensure right outputs and receive appropriate ROI.

When a Technical Person of Indian Origin Shifts to India from the Parent Company

When the company decides to send a person from the parent company, its first choice would normally be a person of Indian origin. Not surprisingly, even the returning Indian, having stayed abroad for a long time, will find a big gap between the current ground reality and his previous work experience in India—if any—of years past. He will discover many issues that were either non-existent in the past or did not have a major impact on the work environment, but which have become a major concern now. For example, the increased awareness of discrimination and harassment, the high challenges of recruitment and attrition, adhering to the Information Technology Act, working from home, and so on are as common to the India market too as they were back "home." Similarly, many old issues are no longer valid in the current scenarios.

When a Technical Person of Non-Indian Origin Shifts to India from the Parent Company

This situation is probably the most difficult to allow for success. The person will face multiple challenges such as choosing the city, understanding the government rules and regulations, identifying support activities that need to be outsourced, choosing the outsourcing partners and those who will manage the outsource partners, hiring and building the team, project execution and understanding the Indian industry and its dynamics. All of these will take time and will be a test of patience and perseverance. If the person is determined to hang in for the long term, then there are ways to succeed, for example: from setting the right expectations with the parent company about timelines, desired results, to spending a few initial months on just setting up and streamlining the operations without even bothering about the technical deliverables. Once the basic infrastructure is in place, through the establishment of a very good set of advisors in the non-technical areas (either by hiring or by outsourcing), the person in charge can start concentrating on building the technical team and delivering the product.

The other option is to hire people who are good general managers and hand over the operations to them, in order to focus on building a stronger technical team. This model can work as long as there is a clear distinction of the responsibility and accountability between them to avoid two power centers. Over time, this delegation of responsibilities can also help the person hand over the technical aspect to the local team and return to the parent company.

A General Manager Coming from the Parent Company

Sending in a person with general management experience was very prevalent in the last two decades when the senior management pool in India was scarce. As the Indian industry has matured, one can find very good people to head operations. However, a few large organizations still prefer sending in talent from the parent company.

For a startup or a young company, where time is always at a premium, this model takes far too much time to allow for success in a short time frame.

A General Manager Hired Locally

Hiring a senior talent with general management experience is now a common exercise by many organizations. This option provides many benefits, such as familiarity with the compensation structure and benefits prevailing in the industry, ability to handle complicated people management issues that usually occur with local industry scenarios and culture, and an understanding of the social fabric of society and the personal circumstances of the people hired. This person should not only be knowledgeable about the country's specific rules and regulations, but also should possess good contacts within the industry to help resolve generic issues or conduct a good recruitment and provide the right perspective on a given situation to the parent organization.

Nevertheless, this alone is not enough. A local hire can only be successful if a technical person from the parent company can work together with the hire for the initial period. This person will help in ramping up the initial technical team, increase the competency level of the team, and become a bridge between the parent company and the

Indian operations in propagating the parent company vision, mission and culture. After an initial period, several technical people, who can travel to India on rotation to achieve goals, can split this role.

It is better to hire the general management person from the same technology domain because in the end, the person has to manage the technology and be responsible for the deliverables of the team, both of which will continue to grow.

It is best if the local management leader could spend 60-80% of their time setting up multiple activities for the new organization like Finance, Administration, HR laws, Legal, IT, Recruitment, brand building, culture setting, etc. (even though some of these will be outsourced). During the second year, this percentage can be reduced to around 30%.

A Sales/Marketing Person Hired Locally or Shifted from the Parent Company

As the Indian industry continues to grow and a few customers turn early adopters of new technology, it is an ideal environment for a small company to setup sales and marketing functions together with the development center. Although this scenario is common in large companies, it is a growing phenomenon in the past couple of years even for small businesses.

The local sales person will have an advantage over the person from the parent company because he has better contacts in the target customer segment, which could definitely help in closing deals. On the other hand, the person from the parent company might have a better understanding of the product and hence might make an effective sale by providing a larger perspective to the client.

The challenge in both cases will be to provide a uniform company culture across the teams to avoid working in silos. On the contrary, development and sales/marketing teams being co-located will provide better coordination in product definition and execution and therefore will provide a faster response to the customers.

The dilemma does not end here.

Scope of Responsibility

There are numerous questions as to whom the head of India operations will report to. Here are some frequently discussed options on reporting, which will be discussed later in this chapter.

* To the CEO

* To the COO

* To Program Management office

* To an Engineering VP

* To a Sales/Marketing VP

This decision is somewhat easy initially, when there is only one operation setup. In this case, the India head reports to the sponsor—the person responsible for setting up the India office. However, when other operations in the parent company also choose to setup their own teams in India, it becomes a complex issue. Some organizations have a multifaceted matrix reporting structure. They have geographical (Asia Pacific or South Asia, or South East Asia) and/ or functional (support, engineering, sales, marketing) report orders, which can make it complicated and beyond the scope of discussion here.

It is important to look into the responsibilities of the India head that will decide the reporting structure.

The first and foremost objective is to run and grow the operation. This consists of two major components: the main functions (e.g. manufacturing, product development, validation, back office support etc.) and support functions (legal, finance, Admin, HR, and IT, etc.)

In some cases, the India head is an administrator looking after support functions, in addition to handling government relations, press and brand building. In other cases, an India head will take on the marketing and sales function along with the support functions. Some of the India heads will have a couple of execution teams to manage and provide support directly to other execution teams (managed by another manager, linked by "dotted lines" to the India head).

For a very large organization (over 1000 people or so), one cannot avoid having multiple divisions headed by division heads. In these cases, either one administrative head will provide support to division heads or one of the division heads will take additional responsibility of handling support functions and act as India head too. In the large organization where support functions are "shared services", these shared services provide support to the center head in running the operations, freeing him or her from the day-to-day support responsibilities.

Nevertheless, the most important aspect for the center head of a small or medium organization or for the division head of a large organization in India is to make sure that the various execution teams should not work in silos. It is important that the India head or division head (as appropriate) take up the responsibility for execution from all divisions (if working on the same product line) and work together with the respective division/team heads in providing a smooth execution. Such a leader will definitely require senior help in providing daily implementation and flexibility in movement of peoples and physical resources in order to achieve better utilization and to save some of the critical projects that suffer from scarcity of good resources. This will also promote better knowledge sharing.

Whom should the India head report to? There is no simple answer, but the basic philosophy of reporting is that the position should facilitate smooth execution and information should flow smoothly, providing minimum decision-making hierarchies and linking the India operation efficiently with the other operations around the world.

One important aspect in this reporting discussion is that many Human Resources Information system (HRIS) software packages work for "solid line" reporting. In many organizations, the India head will not have everyone in India reporting to them, and therefore the system will hinder the India head in providing a unifying policy across teams.

Choosing the Right Leader Summarized:

It is important to remember that one size does not fit all. The company should do a self-assessment on its vision, mission and charter. It also needs to examine not only its short-term expectations and long-term strategies, but also its expectation from the leader, skills brought in by an expatriate and skills supplemented through local hiring. The company should be patient enough to find the right person even though it may take several months. It is crucial to find a strong leader who can build a stronger team and deliver better-than-expected results.

Choosing the Right Leader Case Studies:

Case 2.1: I need to setup a center in India since we are discussing various projects for execution in India. My management has asked me to elect a person who has the right balance of technical and general management skills. The person should possess great communication skills and his past records should prove that he has built or scaled a team of a hundred or more people. My company does not even have a sales office in India, and as a privately held company, it does not have a brand. I am convinced that I should recruit the person from India and not have to transfer someone from the US. I will exploit my network to find out a competent person to take up this role. I have a couple of leads and I have received a few more from recruiters. After interviewing candidates for nearly five months, I realize that good candidates are attracted to established brands for their stability and if they do accept a position with a smaller company, they expect a very high remuneration. Some initially accept the offer and later on have turned it down for some reason. I am tempted to shelve the idea of finding the appropriate leader, even issuing a half page ad in the newspaper does not help and even the recruiters who place executives are unable to provide the right resumes.

How shall I find a leader?

Case 2.2: The management asked a person of Indian origin to relocate to India. He is very happy to take up this opportunity. He came for a brief visit with his family to get a feel of the city and looked for schools to admit his children and to inquire about the right location for the office and house. On his return, he decided to make a move to India. He has setup the expectation with the parent company that it might take him six months to setup the office and form the core team. Once he moved to India, he had to work extremely hard to settle his family down, find office space, and set up a recruitment process. Though he outsourced most of the activities, he still had to follow up with every vendor. All these activities took a toll, and at the end of six months, when he could not see the desired results, he wanted to handover this role to his replacement from the U.S. and transfer back to the U.S.

What might have gone wrong?

Case 2.3: A person of non-Indian origin comes to India to setup the India operations. He is primarily a technical person and wants to setup the offshore center for his team. He is excited that he is pioneering the setup. If successful, other directors will also leverage his setup to form their own respective teams. The U.S. Company supports him, provides a good expatriate package and sets up some milestones for his role.

The person starts receiving leads to agencies that can help in setting operations, from friends and colleagues in the US. After a few months, he realizes that he cannot set up the operation and simultaneously make the team productive to deliver the solution as easily as he expected. He suggests hiring a senior person under him who can execute general management. His supervisor understands the problem and suggests the following:

> "I agree with your suggestion, but it would be better if this person reports directly to me, so that by the time you return in a couple of years, he can be groomed to drive technical deliverables too."

> The person ponders this and finally seeing some merit in it agrees to proceed in that direction.

The general manager is hired and starts working together with the expat technical head. At times, the general manager feels that the technical head is overbearing and is free with suggestions where his expertise is unnecessary. On the other hand, the technical head feels that it is his responsibility to induct the general manager into the overall company culture and therefore, he should share his thoughts with him.

Slowly, the organization moves towards two power centers:

If you are the supervisor of these two people, what will you do?

3 Setting up the Operation

In the process of setting up an India operation, the first decision to make is to decide whether to setup an independent operation of the company or to outsource it to a service company.

Outsource or Offshore

Many organizations setup their own operations outside the country of origin, called off shoring. Other large service companies provide help in setting up the operations called outsourcing. There are many advantages to outsourcing. Most of the times these two terms are used interchangeably.

Upon defining the scope of the work and mutually agreeing upon the modus operandi of the execution with the selected service company, the onus of execution shifts to the outsourcing company. They allocate space, form the team and manage the project. They also handle all people management issues.

One reason this is an ideal scenario is that the organization does not want to add headcount to its payroll because the project would be of short duration or that there is only a need for a certain number of people at various phases of the execution. No company wants to hire people knowing that after a certain period, the management will eventually dismiss their services.

When the organization wants to engage its own people in the core functions alone, outsourcing becomes an ideal option. In this case, the company outsources the noncore activities, such as supporting a product line that is going to be obsolete in the near future.

Sometimes, in order to kick-start a new project, a company requires some of the resources immediately with a specific background. Service companies have a large list of clients that might include competition and can immediately provide the required skill.

Though there is no industry data to prove whether offshore centers are cost effective to outsource operation or vice versa; based on unofficial data no one has any significant cost advantages.

A lot of planning is required to make an outsourcing option feasible. Planning is required to determine the size of the team and its composition. Detailed attention and focus is required in specifying the work to be outsourced. Considerations about the type of process to use, status-reporting mechanism, risk analysis, escalation of issues, tools required for the project and other factors are also very important. The type of training and its frequency associated with a travel plan (the engineers need to travel abroad or a team of instructors will travel to India) is also required.

In spite of the many advantages to outsourcing, many companies still prefer to establish an India offshore center. The reasons behind this decision could be multifold.

The first and most important decision to make is whether the move to India is a strategic or tactical decision. Outsourcing is typically a tactical decision to get around the issues at hand, while offshoring is a strategic decision in alignment with the company's growth plan.

The talent and level of skills that the client company requires would define the beginning of an outsourcing relationship. This decision is usually a result of doing a gap analysis of clients' existing resource pool and identifying the additional resource requirements. If during the execution, the talent set needs revision, the service partner must be willing to adapt (mostly by charging a premium).

The service companies usually ask their clients to choose the core team by selecting from a set of resumes and briefly interviewing the short listed candidates. However, this is normally limited to the formation of the core team. The management team of the service company chooses the other team members. There is a limitation with this approach, as you are either not given free hand in choosing the rest of the team, or do not have time to do it, or you have to compromise based on the resumes you get. This will lead to a formation of a team, which might not be what you had envisioned.

The resource movement is high within the service company. People can move out due to their own career planning, seed other projects for a different client; also, there may be no space for a given role in the existing team. At times, the scope of work in the service company is not end-to-end. Hence, some of the early people who joined the team would not get an opportunity to contribute in the later phases. This will lead to moving out to other client projects, resulting in the dilution of the knowledge base initially built. This will also add an extra burden when training new resources (though owned by the service company). Often, this becomes a delay in moving up the value chain to take more ownership.

Technology companies pay keen attention to intellectual property. Small companies or startups with one or two product lines in their pre-launch stage will have issues in sharing product knowledge with the service company. The outsourcing does provide the necessary safeguard, but it remains an outside organization. Clearly stating that the ownership of patents generated during the execution in the agreement is important to avoiding any misunderstanding later.

Execution of the project will also pose challenges. If the agreement is to allow service companies to use their own development process and quality metrics, then rolling them to the client's master database is a problem. On the other hand, if the outsourcing partner follows the same process and uses the same tools the client does, then the cost of the tools must be addressed within the contract.

Setting up one's own offshore center will exact virtually the same cost advantages. The cost for the human resource is up to 75% of the expense in any software company in India. In that case, it is of no concern whether the work is outsourced or offshored. The offshore center will have a higher human cost if the average experience level of the team is higher than the outsourcing partner provides.

In general, smaller medium product organizations have preferred to open their own offshore centers, while the business units of the large organizations take their own independent decisions whether to go for an outsourcing partner or to establish their own offshore center. In some cases, they go for a combination of both. It is also true that sometimes small or medium companies will not have large requirements (as far as numbers are concerned) and therefore, they fear not getting proper management focus from the outsourcing partners.

Once the decision to setup an offshore center is finalized, there are various ways to proceed with its establishment. There are many companies available to help in setting up the operations—from fulfilling government formalities, to identifying the facility and recruiting personnel. There are incubators who provide space for entrepreneurs and small organizations until a decision for a full-fledged center is established.

Choosing the Right City

Location is a major consideration in deciding the India office. Many factors play a role in deciding the city.

Cost

A Cushman Wakefield report[6] published in March of 2006 provides the rental landscape for major cities in India. This report forecasts the rental values based on economic variables influencing the commercial hubs. Author's interpretation of this report, by using rents in Bangalore

---

6. Office snapshot Chennai, Bangalore, Hyderabad, New Delhi, Pune: Cushman & Wakefield India Private Limited.

(Central Business District) as a base figure; Gurgaon (near Delhi), Pune and Chennai will be about 20% cheaper, while Hyderabad will be around 35-40% cheaper. The commerce districts of New Delhi will be 2 to 3 times costlier than Bangalore, while Mumbai business areas will be approximately 4-5 times costlier.

The peripheral areas will be around 20-40% cheaper in comparison to the center. There is not much significant difference in rental among Bangalore, Hyderabad, Chennai and Pune as far as peripheral areas are concerned.

In addition to the rental cost, the cost of living differs from city to city. Government employees receive differential allowances based on the cost of living in different cities. It is probably best to assume the same salary requirements for most of the India centers.

There are a few reasons for this: One of the primary reasons is that it can act as an incentive to move to a low cost city. As a result, the center will also grow and in turn, help the operation from a cost perspective. Second, people seeking transfer or a temporary position could take place in a location that helps in project execution; therefore, keeping the same salary is good from an administrative viewpoint. A third reason could be that the delta is not large enough to add to the administrative cost of maintaining differential pay.

For BPO (Business Process Outsourcing) industries, the cost factor is a primary influencer which will lead them to choose either tier-2 or tier-3 cities.

Talent Pool Availability

Depending upon the requirements, companies find most of the talent either from educational institutes or from existing industries.

As mentioned in chapter one, a key factor that lead to the growth of Bangalore in the early eighties was the large number of technical brains who left Government defense jobs and joined IT companies. From this, we see that the readily available pool of people is necessary.

Indian Government statistical figures[7] state that the country has around 14,000 institutes of higher learning, which churn out around 440,000 technical graduates every year. This figure should not lead one to think that there is an extraordinary large pool of talent available in India. According to a Frost and Sullivan report[8], sponsored by the India Semiconductor Association (ISA), less than 1,500 graduates specialize annually in the VLSI (Very large-scale integration). Companies should consider the domain expertise area while choosing to open the offshore center. There is no specific domain-wise data available in each city. For example, most companies specializing in telecom software development are still located in Bangalore. Although other cities do have companies working in that domain, they are not near the numbers located in Bangalore.

It is also possible to begin operations in one city and launch another product development in another city, as the resources might be more readily available in that city. Some large organizations follow this method of expansion.

Similarly, for setting up a small company that requires a specific skill set, it is easy to decide on any tier-2 city where talent is available in sufficient numbers, reducing the risk of loosing them to competitors. This is especially true for strengths of less than 50 (ideally, 10-20 people setup). This can be a niche R&D type of project, wherein talent pool availability does not matter much.

If it is possible for a project to be executed with a team of a few senior members working together with fresh hires, then consider the talent resource availability from a large number of engineering colleges. Currently, there is a moderately good spread of engineering colleges across India, albeit not uniform. As per STPI, around 10% of engineering graduates come from Karnataka (the state where Bangalore is located), but students can study in any college in India. Although some graduates prefer to work close to their native home, most of them are flexible in migrating to another city.

---

7. http://en.wikipedia.org/wiki/All_India_Council_for_Technical_Education
8. http://www.isaonline.org/documents/isafns_report_execsum.pdf

Political Environment & Infrastructure

This is also a critical criterion for choosing a city. Most of the regions in India are conducive for setup. Even though central/federal government policies are uniform in the country, various states do compete in getting foreign investments.

The type of setup also determines the dependence of a decision, often arrived upon the incentives provided from the state government. If one were setting up a manufacturing unit then the supply of water, electricity along with their price would play an important role.

The size of the operation also matters. If one has a plan to setup a big operation or has future expansion plans and intends to buy land for it, then state government incentives will be most beneficial.

India is a democratic country and elections keep changing the government. More often than not, the current government tends to honor the commitments of the previous government in regards to IT companies.

Several other factors also play a pivotal role: accessibility to international airports, good roads for fast commuting, efficient public transport, easy customs handling facilities, uninterrupted availability of electricity, and high bandwidth connectivity to parent companies together with a backup route.

If you are not the early bird in a city, you can meet with the existing companies and learn from their experiences, which can help you in making the right decisions.

Miscellaneous

Many other factors are involved in deciding which city to establish a base of operations. Sometimes, the company requires close cooperation with a specific university or college and being co-located is an advantage. If the product is custom-made for Indian consumers, the target audience's location is the de-facto choice for close cooperation. Likewise, if the center has to work closely with a Government institution or a laboratory, then it is practical to select the same city.

For a person of Indian origin in the parent company who is responsible for setting up operations, sometimes a city near to his native home is preferred.

A favorable climatic condition can also be an added advantage, but is not a major consideration.

As mentioned above, various factors can influence a decision. It also depends on the requirements and the associated priorities assigned to the various factors in choosing the most desirable location. Say, the ASIC Design and Verification Company in the US wants to setup an R&D facility in India. Initially they want to start with a small number of say 20-30 people, but have plans to expand to a 100 or more. In addition, the company is to be listed on the US Stock Market. In this situation, there are many approaches that can be adopted, but the commonly used approach is to look for other companies in the same domain i.e. ASIC and find out the location in India. One would find that there are companies in Bangalore, Hyderabad and Pune doing work in ASIC. The next step would be to find out the size of the setups in these cities and the types of projects they execute. Normally, one will find that the larger setups are in Bangalore, whereas cities such as Pune or Hyderabad tend to have smaller setups. In this case, the decision would most likely drive them to an establishment in Bangalore.

If cost is a major criterion and the anticipated growth in headcount is moderate, then Pune and Hyderabad would be far more accommodating.

Now let us say that the company wants to focus entirely on R&D and is looking for a tie up with a premium university. In this case, they will choose people from a premium institution and locate the office in the city where the institute is located.

To take the discussion further, if the ASIC Company is developing the chip in partnership with a customer in New Delhi, then a practical choice is to open the office in New Delhi for better coordination.

In another example, say the parent company wants to setup a small team for product development where a few senior members from the parent company can shift to India and work with less experienced or fresh graduates. The company does not require any large lab or setup because completion of work simply requires a few laptops and PCs. In this case, any tier2 cities near the premium institution having the facilities like "export zones", would be an ideal choice for setup. Not only is this conducive from a cost perspective, but also from a hiring and retention viewpoint as well.

Once the city is decided, the next step is selecting the location within the city and planning the facility.

Choosing the Facility

Choosing the right location within the city is important for all kinds of companies, but is most critical for a small operation (less than 200 people). It is better to choose a locale somewhere inside the city, so that the average commuting time can be reduced. If the parent company is a startup or it is not well known, then the location within the city can play a factor in attracting the right talent. Large organizations having more than 1,000 people can establish themselves in outskirts of a city, as they will be able to run their own transportation from various part of the city for the convenience of their employees.

The other decision, which the company needs to take, is whether to rent the facility or to purchase it. Normally, this is a corporate-level decision. Most companies prefer a rental facility. In any case, it best to keep the following guidelines in mind:

Legal documents of the land ownership and the compliance with building by-laws are necessary to avoid any legal hassles later on. Once important paperwork clears the company from a legal angle, one can proceed to get the lease documents prepared for rental. It is preferable to get the lease agreement registered with the government.

Various terms and conditions are city specific. There is something called a "lock-in" period. The term "lock-in" means that you cannot vacate the premises during this period. If you want to vacate, you have to pay the rent up to the "lock-in" period. It is better to get a clause of "right to sub-lease", so that if you want to move out in between the "lock-in" period, you can put it up for rent. (A word of caution that you need to verify with Tax and Audit advisors: As the purpose of setup is for software export, by sub-leasing the facility, one appears to be in real estate business. Therefore, it is important to follow proper steps, such as making sure that there is no difference in rent paid and the rent received). This "lock-in" period is negotiable and is more common in new buildings.

Some builders require a "Security Deposit". This term refers to a multiple of monthly rentals that one needs to pay as a lump sum at the time of contract signing. Upon the end of the lease period, one will receive the "security deposit" without interests. Normal wear and tear is fine, but any major faults usually come from the security deposit, unless the tenant rectifies it on their own or pays separately.

Parking charges and maintenance charges for common areas or amenities are either included in the rental or paid separately. Electricity and other utility charges are determined and paid according to the usage.

There are two types of rentals: Bare Shell and Fully furnished. In the case of bare-shell rentals, one pays monthly rental only for the bare shell facility. The responsibility of doing the interior is based on individual requirement. With fully furnished options, the builder will do the interior and add markup to the rental. In a new facility, the builder can make the interior based on the client's requirements. For facilities that are not new, either the tenant pays for the modifications or the builder makes the changes. In the latter case, the builder can ask for a one-time payment or can markup the rental further.

If the power situation is not 24/7, then almost all the facilities will have a generator facility that the builder provides. Normally, the tenant is responsible for UPS and EPBX installations.

It is important that the builder clearly discuss the "renewal of lease" clause and "escalation of rent". It is standard practice in any given city.

There are various types of buildings available on the market. Many companies follow their corporate policies in designing the interior and adhere to a particular checklist. In all cases, fire alarms, extinguishers, emergency exits and other basic security features are important considerations.

If one is planning to setup a telecom laboratory or manufacturing units etc., then an experienced person in India or from the parent company must supervise and facilitate the projects in tier-1 cities.

The facilities in India are modern with all the latest amenities, depending upon business requirements. Services can be fully wireless, having CCTV, public address system etc.

Some large companies provide additional facilities like day-care, health clubs, recreation centers, libraries, etc.

Upon deciding on the city and the facility, one needs to start working on the formation of the company and compliance with various government regulations mentioned in Appendix A.

Formation of the Support Team (HR, Finance, Admin and IT)

In the past, whether to outsource or keep these functions in-house was a source of major debate. Recently, the trend has become to outsource these functions. Some of the organizations outsource their full activities to external agencies. These agencies station one or two people at the client location to coordinate. While other companies hire a skeleton team to manage these external agencies. The second seems a better approach for a simple reason: these functions are very critical to the success of the organization and having employees running and managing the show provides a greater sense of ownership and comfort in handling a company's confidential data.

In the case of small setups, say less than 100 employees, one may need to have 3-4 people on the support team. They should have expertise in one area, but must also be acquainted in others. For example, one can find people with any of the combinational skills: Admin and IT, Admin and Finance, Finance and HR or Admin and HR. Therefore, one should put in an effort to ensure hiring the most talented and experienced people for these roles, just like any other domain role (e.g. engineering). As they will be a one-person-army in their own function, they should have a great grasp on their subject matter. Issues may come up in regards to vacations, but that tends to be easily rectifiable. Normally, a person from the support team can do some basic troubleshooting or follow up. If the issue is more severe, then it is best to arrange help from the outsourced company. Another important quality required for these roles is a high standard for, "Ethics". Ethics are required for every person in the organization; but the bar is set higher for them as they handle external agencies.

As the organization grows, one could have a small team for each focused area in support.

Please see Appendix B for vendor management guidelines needed by the support team.

By now, the guidelines about costs required to setup and run the operation should be clear. Based on this information, one needs to determine the India budget. Normally, a change in budget can occur due to two reasons: First, expansion plans of the facility linked with the hiring plan and second, an unexpected salary hike due to market pressure. The expansion plan is normally coordinated with the parent company's desire and therefore they will understand this, but the salary hike is a local issue and this requires lots of answering to the parent company. It is important to explore this aspect.

Salary Hikes and Escalation of Cost

This is one of the most discussed topics in the hot job market. More and more companies are coming to India. Any new company planning to set up their operation needs to attract the right talent, and one of the main ways to attract talent is to pay more. Supply and demand drive the salary hike.

If you are setting up the operation, it is better to start by hiring some senior people. Let us take a simple example:

Year X end: There are 50 people in the company having an average experience level of 5 years, assuming the salary is USD 25K per engineer per year.

Year X+1 beginning: one decides to give 20% hike

During Year X+1: The 50 people are now averaging 5 years (which will become six by the end of this year) of experience and will cost USD 30K per engineer per year.

In the same year, one adds 50 more people with an average of 3 years (which will become 4 by the end of this year) of experience and with a salary of USD 20K per engineer per year (as per new salary chart).

End of Year X+1: you will have 100 people with average 5 years of experience having USD 25K per engineer per year.

This is simple mathematics, but it is definitely effective to convince the parent organization that yearly salary hikes may not correspond to the same increase in cost. There are a few stipulations involved, which may be applicable to growing organizations only. In reality, there will be fluctuations in cost. The cost sampling will vary at a given time depending upon the hiring pattern, the hiring numbers and the experience mix.

The other factor that can help to counter balance salary hikes is seeing the increased value in the output coming out from India operations. Great examples of this include taking more ownership during the expanded scope of a product development life cycle, by being more independent in resolving issues and taking more initiative in applying best practices along with producing better quality output.

Here we will discuss what could be the scope of work in India.

Choosing the Right Work

The organization needs to consider the activities needed to execute in India.

The first question to ask should be "Is the management in charge of setting up the India operation or starting a new project at the offshore center committed to making it a success?"

If the parent company is not fervently committed, but is forced into offshoring for various reasons such as: cost-saving, or a push from upper management or that there is simply no other option but to try it out, then the first response will be to "test the water." A "testing the water" approach will take far too long and will most likely not be successful.

The offshore centers adopt various approaches. Listed below are some common approaches:

Back-office: Some offshore centers focus only on back-office activities in India, while other centers combine back-office activities with their mainline activities. Normally, these two operations are separate because the skill sets are somewhat different. As a result, transfer of personnel between the two is uncommon.

Maintenance Project: In this case, one starts with the maintenance project, which is not critical for the company. This will provide time for the management in the parent company to understand and learn about Indian operations. Such an operation takes off without considering the strategy for an India center. In such a situation, word is bound to spread fast in the job market that the work is not challenging, which usually leads to hesitation on part of the exceptional talent to apply. Due to lack of the right talent on the team, the desired result might not come or will come later than expected. The parent company will use this experience in their decision-making (on what type of project should be offshored) and will continue to execute projects considered lower in value. Even though a company has a globally known brand, people will not flock to it if the work content is not good. In the end this could affect a company's image and was a practice that was far more prevalent in the past.

A mix of maintenance, new feature development and test projects: Some companies try a different strategy. They create a roadmap and share it with prospective hires. With this approach, they start with the maintenance project and add new feature developments for the same product line after a couple of quarters. They implement job rotations, so that their people can experience a mix of both worlds. Similarly, they also implement this for the test team, wherein they mix old feature regression and new feature testing. A word of caution on this approach is that the initially presented and promised plan given to the team should also follow the timeline promised. When informed accordingly, many people will wait and will understand the delay as long as it is within acceptable limits.

The other approach followed by some companies is to have two separate teams in two separate divisions or under separate senior management. The formation of these two teams might be at different timeline or concurrent. If one of the teams is having pure maintenance work and other one is having a new feature development work, then one cannot avoid team members of one team asking for a transfer to the next team. This should be handled well and should be stated clearly under the company guidelines (It can decide on protocol for internal transfers, or if transfer is allowed only after two years of service or as positions become open and anyone can apply and be interviewed together with external candidates and so on). Normally, transfers are easier intra-division rather than inter division.

Expanded Ownership in the Execution Cycles: Some companies have their system engineering functions and/or their product management functions in India together with development functions. Some offshore centers that have responsibilities for limited phases of execution also have increased ownership of other phases. Some centers have extended test facilities to test significant parts of the product and/or make a release from India.

Full or significant ownership of old Product line: This will provide a good exposure to the product development lifecycle and improve the skill set of employees. The team will be excited to be a part of this. Excitement increases if a good number of active customers patronize the product line and ask for new features ever so often.

Full or significant ownership of a new product line: This normally happens in startups or with small- to medium-sized companies. This can also happen to newly formed business units in a large company. If a company manufactures the product only for India or the Asian market, then the decision to do it in India is practical. Sometimes, due to a merger and acquisition, some new products are incorporated into the portfolio and the parent company transfers it to India. A good number of companies operate with a skeleton team (mostly sales, technical marketing etc.) at the parent company and full product development, product management and support team in India.

In some companies, the recruitment starts in anticipation of the new project. Sometimes, people join the company, but wait for several months for the clarity of work content and proper work assignment. This leads to frustration, making it counterproductive for both the people and the company. In extreme cases, people start resigning even before the start of the work itself.

Setting up the Operation Summarized:

As stated earlier, the Indian industry is no longer young. It is mature and prepared to take on higher challenges. Sponsor teams of the parent company will have to undertake frequent travels to India, take conference calls at odd hours and invest a significant effort to ensure that the Indian team understands every detail of the product. The more effort one puts in the beginning, the better and faster results one could expect from the Indian center. This is in the larger interest of the company, which has to be in conjunction with the excellent hiring and smooth execution, as discussed in the following chapters.

Setting up the Operation Case Studies:

Case 3.1: A product development company wants to setup an India offshore center. The search for the center head is taking much longer than anticipated, which has prompted the head of engineering and finance to plunge into setting the operations or else the product development might be delayed. The head of HR is against proceeding without first hiring the India head. Gradually, the HR head agrees to proceed with the setup and hiring while concurrently searching a leader. They manage to find a facility and hire a few engineers. After a few months, you join as the center head.

On your very first day, the engineering head calls you from the US and welcomes you. He says that the first important activity you need to carry out is recruitment. As far as an HR position in India is concerned, unfortunately, the requisition is not approved and therefore you can utilize the US HR head for any clarification. She will be calling you by the end of your day. He also mentions that G&A (General and Administration) is not correctly set up, a matter which has to be taken up with the HR and Finance.

After the call is over, you meet with the people who are already part of the team. They seem happy and quote, "It is good that you are on board. We have been hearing names, but no one showed up. As much as we hate to give you this letter today, you need to address this list of open issues from our side."

You go through the long list of issues.

Salary is incorrect or not deposited on time; Medical insurance is lousy; the Travel policy is not clear and travel to US is imminent. There is no transportation facility and it becomes difficult to work late hours. There is no cafeteria facility for lunch. Library and Gym facilities are also missing.

You tell them that you will look into the high priority issues first. You also mention to them that your first priority is to put things in order.

It is already evening and the expected phone call from HR in the US comes through. She says that it is better to write an employee handbook and setup travel, leave and medical insurance policies. She adds that she is sending the ones available in the US to ensure consistency. She also suggests prioritizing this task before you take up any other activities.

To your surprise, the last phone call of the day comes from the Finance head. He says that you need to finalize the facility lease agreement, even though we have moved, and line up the accounting and audit firm. He has doubts on vendor management from contract and deliverables perspective. He tells you to focus your first priority in putting all the legal aspects in order.

You need to accomplish four different tasks, but all team heads are asking you to look into their own priorities first.

If quitting is not an option, what will you do?

Case 3.2: Murali is a person of Indian origin who has completed his bachelors in India and masters in US. He is working at Company XYZ in the San Francisco bay area, but gets the opportunity to setup an India offshore center for his company to build a team who can work together with US team on new product line with state-of-the-art technology. The company is currently outsourcing the maintenance of one of their products in Bangalore with a service company for many years. The company decides to relocate Murali and his family for good. Murali is excited not only about this opportunity, but also about getting more visibility and job security by taking up this position, where as in Bay area he had recently started fearing job loss, as the product on which he is working was to be shelved soon.

Murali is a natural technical person with no background in general management. He is excited but nervous too. His comfort zone is to fall towards resolving technical issues, which has hindered him in not putting a right focus on general management that resulted in passing any issue in that area to US for guidance, clarification or decision.

Suddenly, he receives feedback from his supervisor that the HR and Finance authorities were complaining that some of the decisions that he should have taken locally are coming to them. They also cribbed that Murali should be on top of issues by suggesting solutions. There are pending issues that are still not closed e.g. What are the ways to get the money back in the US, which is piling up in India, due to transfer pricing?

The supervisor advises Murali, to think whether he would like to continue in this position or would want to move to a purely technical one. His supervisor suggests that he can convince his management to open a requisition for a senior position. If that happens, then he needs to decide about his reporting.

What should Murali do?

4 Recruitment Challenges

Recruitment plays one of the most critical and vital roles in making a company successful. Costs for human capital is very high in IT and IT enabled service industry. This is not the case with other engineering industries where capital cost is significant because of equipment, raw material and transportation. The movement of people makes the IT industry and other skilled labor related industry much more susceptible. The solution is to put more focus on hiring the right talent and retaining them. Half the battle is won if a dream team can be assembled. It is possible to build a dream team by spending more time and planning on effective recruitment.

There are five important stages in the recruitment process:

Stage 1: Sourcing

Recruiting Agencies

Recruitment agencies have huge databases of qualified individuals. They can help with media advertising, short-listing of suitable candidates and streamlining the interview and selection process. This is useful if you are hiring in large numbers within a very short span of time or doing target hiring for some specific skills where the pool is small.

Some organizations outsource their entire recruitment process to agencies, which is not the best or ideal solution. A small or medium size company may not have a recognized brand compared to established organizations; this could mean that the employer is in a better position to "sell" a prospective employee rather than the recruiting agencies.

Some organization go for a hybrid model, where they have their own team for recruitment and take the help of recruiting agencies for specific skill sets.

When hiring in large numbers, the attention to detail and quality could be lost. If the employer ends up doing most of the work in the hiring process, then the cost in retaining a recruiting agency is pointless. On the other hand, some recruitment agencies will go the extra mile to get a good team in place. The organization should be prepared to pay a premium for such services and should dedicate a portion of its staff to work with them to provide all help and support for a quick and precise decision.

Referrals

Referrals are one of the best sources for hiring. Many companies pay referral bonuses to their employees on successful hires based on their referrals. One can extend the referral scheme to those who have accepted the offer, but have not yet joined by giving them the referral bonus once they join.

"High confidence referrals" are when the existing employees know the candidate that has a good understanding of the company. The referring employee will know the job requirement well and chances of a good match are high. They will also be familiar with the work culture, which will help them in providing the right perspective to the prospective employee. This reduces the effort and time of the interview process.

"Medium confidence referrals" are when the employee does not know the person, but merely passes the candidate's resume received from some other source.

"Low confidence referrals" are when you can get only a phone number or email address through the employee. One should make sure that the employee has consented with the candidate before providing the phone number or email address.

Sometimes, significant effort is required to get the resume to proceed with the interview process.

Newspaper Advertisements

Even though web portals are challenging the effectiveness of newspaper advertisements, it still helps to spread the word. In the past, newspaper ads were one of the major and most effective sources of recruitment, but the percentage of employees joining through newspaper advertisements has reduced.

Depending upon the company and its skill requirements, one can receive anywhere in the range of 1000 to 10000+ resumes from a single advertisement. Though it is difficult to quantify the hit ratio, only around 1% of the resumes are normally worth calling for interviews. Out of the candidates interviewed, the company might select only 10% of them. These numbers can fluctuate depending on the domain, experience level and organizational requirements.

Portals

In the high technology hiring realm, portals have broken the advertising monopoly that newspapers used to enjoy. Portals have become one of the major players and a great contributor in sourcing good resumes.

There have been many mergers happening in portal space, which helps both employer and candidate to concentrate on a few large ones. Portals have come out with far more innovative and accessible approaches to posting jobs and resumes. Not only do they keep their search engine upgraded to provide better and faster results for employers, they also provide various features for managing short listed resumes for employers.

You can choose the usage model that works best for you – portals offer choice of duration, pricing and features. You can make it out within a few days, dependent on whether sufficient fresh and quality resumes were added since the last review. The same portal can provide better results at a given point of time, but may not be of much use at some other timeline. Certain industry events (consolidation, project cancellation, etc.) can provide instant resume boost in the portal. Therefore, it is important to take a snapshot once in a quarter, or based on specific knowledge of the industry.

Keeping an Eye on Your Industry

Full knowledge of your industry e.g. competitors, suppliers, companies working in similar technology areas can be turned into significant aid in recruitment.

Recruitment agencies make unsolicited calls to people in various organizations that meet your requirements, but it is best to avoid such types of calls from the organization. HR should contact candidates only when their resume is received through the proper channels.

Campus Hiring:

On-campus recruiting can be effective under these circumstances:

- When some specific skills are required in new technology (MS/PhD students)

- When you are limited by the cost, and hence decide to go for fresh hires as they will be less expensive

- When you require a large number of fresh hires to populate the bottom of the pyramid in a growing organization

- When you can afford to train new hires for several months before they become productive

- When no direct work experience is required for specific jobs

- When you can predict your hiring plan 8-9 months in advance

- When you can afford to have some fraction of the offers end up being "no-shows" (many college grads end up going for higher studies or receive multiple offers)

- When you can afford to lose them in around 2 years (many people change their first job around this period)

Small companies need to consider these things and hence they normally go for experienced people and might target 2+ years of experienced people.

For campus recruitment, a lot of planning is required. One should try to get a good slot at the beginning of an academic session itself, so that one can hire from a good pool of students. Some schools do not allow students to take up more than a couple of jobs on campus. In that case, it is advisable to go early for recruitment and select from a larger pool.

In order to increase the chances of joining, some organizations hire candidates with Masters Degree, as the chances of masters taking up higher studies are slim. A good amount of investment is required in hiring the fresh because training them will add to expenses. It should also be taken into account the amount of time a new hire will need to spend with a mentor or a guide. Fresh graduates will usually take a longer time to deliver.

Rejected Candidates:

Rejected candidates can become good ambassadors of the organization, if they enjoy the hiring process and are excited about the organization's work culture. Treat all candidates with the utmost respect. Word of mouth publicity is powerful and recommendations coming from rejected candidates help the company in a big way by spending less time in convincing prospects.

Company Web Site:

The Company website needs to contain a detailed list of current job opportunities. A well-known company usually gets a better response through their web site, unlike a young company building a brand name.

A website should be easy to navigate and include clear job descriptions with job codes. Job codes provide an effective tool in sorting resumes and directing them to the respective hiring managers.

Reference Checks:

Some companies have outsourced this important aspect of recruitment. Reference checks also provide a good source of resumes.

Reference checks are helpful only when the candidate provides names of the people with whom he/she has previously worked with.

As an ethical HR practice, the employer should never ask the person to apply when one is conducting a reference check. It is human to become curious to know where a colleague has interviewed. A person may get excited and could recommend others to a given position or may even apply for the job himself. This becomes more effective when the employer does reference checks directly.

Stage 2: Screening

This is almost an around the clock process in the job market. One needs to keep an eye on all the sources of resumes and get them screened fast. One needs to contact candidates with haste and schedule their interviews as early as possible.

The HR or recruiting agencies perform the screening of resumes. The screening is based on the following parameter(s):

- Technical skills

- Target company names

- Educational institution names

- Educational qualifications

- Range of years of experience

- Location preference

One can get better results if the hiring manager can search the database together with the HR person, as he will be in a better position to provide various combinations of keywords to achieve a desired result.

For junior positions, one can also check the marks or grades scored in college. If a candidate has changed jobs too frequently then it raises a flag, unless of course the circumstances are beyond a candidate's control e.g. change of location due to family reasons, closing down of a company or the project was cancelled etc.

Sometimes, the format of a resume in India is totally unknown to overseas employers who struggle to make sense of its format. Some organizations use their own format and ask the candidate to fill in the blanks per their guidelines. The fundamental issue is that many resumes in India mention numerous technologies, platforms, programming languages as experience. Some of which the candidate might have merely read about and might not have in-depth knowledge. Separating the actual experience vis-à-vis superficial knowledge in the very beginning itself will help in effective interviewing. It helps to ask for real-life examples from a candidate's work experience to gauge the depth of his/her knowledge.

Stage 3: Interview Process

"The Candidate is King" should be the motto. The candidate should feel comfortable during the interview process. One has to make them feel important and treat them with respect. While setting up the interview, one needs to accommodate the time slot requested by the candidate and should stick to it. The first positive impression leaves a deep imprint in the mind of the candidate, and they can extrapolate on the type of work environment the new company will provide, based on some of these early interactions.

In order to achieve this, the interviewers need training on proper and effective practices that he or she should follow during the interview process. In addition to their technical skills, it best to evaluate the candidate on their soft skills. Sometimes, great individual contributors might not get along well in a large team environment, thus verification of teamwork, communication and flexibility skills are important. In case of any doubt on a candidate's skill(s), one should utilize the opportunity to verify during the reference check.

Various organizations adopt various ways to conduct interviews. Some conduct a written test followed by interviews. Some will have a panel interview; some will have multiple one-on-one interactions. For managers and above, some will have a 360-degree type of interview.

Some of the Common Pitfalls During the Interview Process:

Timings: There are multiple issues in this category. Sometimes there are miscommunications on the date and or time slot. This becomes more prominent during phone interviews when the candidates are from a distant geographical location. It also happens that the candidate has come on time and waits as the interviewer is busy. As mentioned earlier, it is better that the interviewer adjust their own schedule to accommodate candidate time. It is also advisable to stick to the time allotted for the interview so that the candidate can go back on time. It is fair to ask the candidate to come again later, if all the rounds of interviews are yet to be completed.

Compromise: The candidate is just meeting the requirement, and a hiring manager wants to screen some more candidates before taking the call. It is probably best to acknowledge that the secondary list (or people on hold list) does not help. If the overall comments are neutral and if the panel is not confident that even after initial training the person will not be able to deliver the required result, then it is better not to proceed further. Sometimes, hiring managers do proceed if the referral is very strong or has positive feedback through other reliable sources. If the candidate is good, and the hiring manager wants to go screen a few more candidates to select the best, then they should provide the candidate with a timeline as to when they will be notified of employment. One can interview the candidate again after a year or so, after he acquires some more skill suitable for your requirements.

Test Papers: Sometimes people publish the written test paper on the web, based on their memory and hence it is better to keep changing the format and content for each written examination.

Panel Interview: In a panel interview, one needs to avoid the situation where one panelist wants to outwit the candidate or other interviewers. One can overcome this issue by giving the interviewers proper training. In the 360-degree type of interviews, the subordinates do not reach a consensus to choose their leader. To solve this problem, take individual inputs and decide appropriately.

Veto: This right should be reserved for hiring managers or a senior person. Sometimes in multiple rounds of interviews, any particular interviewer can reject the candidate. Discuss this first with the hiring manager to decide on proceeding further or ending the interview process.

Final Decision: Sometimes decision makers do not coordinate comments on time and it usually ends up as a mixed bag. In this case, a hiring manager has to make a call based on the job requirement and the skill he possesses. Conduct an additional interview to probe the weak area(s) mentioned by other interviewers.

It is important to have the HR interview done as well, as this also provides some new information about the candidate. Depending on the company policy, perform reference checks, employment history checks or both. With the gathered information, the hiring manager can make a quick call on the candidate.

Stage 4: Keeping the Communication Channel Open

In a job market, it is common for a candidate to be looking at 2-3 job offers. During this period, it is a challenge to convert the job offer into a real hire. Hence, it is important to keep following up with the candidates who have taken up an offer.

The first few weeks, after resigning from their old organization, is a challenging period for applicants. During this time, the person will go through a cycle of discussions with their employer and come under intense pressure. During this time, some candidates might come back and ask some more probing questions. Providing right answers to his or her concern areas will help in resolving the issue. Sometimes other influencers (friends, spouse and family) may also cause vacillation in the mind of the candidate.

It is vital to understand a candidate's priorities in his or her next job. It might happen that the existing company is willing to fulfill said priority on receiving their resignation letter so that the person may reconsider their withdrawal. It can also happen that another company's package might fulfill his or her priority. Once you understand the priority of the candidate, then you should try to meet his or her expectation within the defined policy of the company. For example, if the person is looking for a couple of short-term overseas assignments as a part of their next job change but you cannot promise this; then it is best to state it upfront. Similarly, if your company has very few hierarchies, and you cannot provide the desired designation to a prospective candidate, it is best to state this up front as well.

Those who remain firm and who have made up their mind can withstand the flurry of emotional and psychological pressures, but for others it is important to keep the channels of communication open. This helps in converting the "Nays" to Ayes". In the end, some will decide not to join even after accepting the offer letter. Sometimes it helps to contact lost candidates after a few months and they might join the company. This might be due to the lack of fulfillment of a promise that the existing company made and could not meet, or that the work and environment in the new company was not up to expectations.

Stage 5: Avoiding Infant Mortality

This step is important; managers should not relax after a person is hired. Some new recruits have joined to test the waters for a couple of days before deciding on really settling down in the company. Therefore, it is important that a proper overview of the product and scope of work is clearly defined for a person to appreciate the challenges. If a lengthy training program is involved before assignment of a project, this will contribute to a new employee's uncertainty. If a new employee does not have a cubicle assigned, a workstation provided, or various accounts, which have yet to open up on day one it will not reflect well on the company's image.

It is advisable for the manager's manager to have a skip level with the new recruit after a couple of weeks to find out any disturbing issue(s), which might be bothering him or her.

Recruitment Challenges Summarized:

The world is flattening and no one has the luxury to run an organization with mediocrity. In a high technology industry with cutthroat competition, one can only win by having an excellent team working together to meet the desired goal. Recruitment is an art and a scientific formula cannot solve employment problems. Therefore, it is important that the right set of people handle recruitment.

Recruitment Challenges Case Studies:

Case 4.1: The Company asks you to shift to India to setup a new project team. Your company is not well known in India, though it has a small offshore center working on few projects in a different domain. The India offshore center also has a medium size back-office operation. You were told that attracting the right talent would be a challenge. You have put an advertisement in the newspaper, but it appears on an unnoticeable page. Yet you receive many responses. After going through them you find out the relevant ones are miniscule in number. You also face a similar experience with the walk-in applicants. You discuss this with your friends and other industry sources. Based on their advice, you send an email to the parent company asking for an increase in the budget allocation for hiring, so that you can take the services of the recruitment firm (where the commission is significant).

You get the approval of the budget and you are happy that the issue was resolved so soon. However, a new situation follows: In-spite of recruiters doing an initial screening and providing required support, you still continue to put a lot of effort in going through the resumes. The ration of meaningful resumes has increased but the timeline in which you are looking to ramp-up the team is looking difficult to meet. Some of the prospects, whom you have short-listed, are not coming for interviews and are asking for a lot of details about the company, the scope of work, career prospects and any overseas travel.

What you should do?

Case 4.2: Taking the above case further, you short list a candidate and want to provide her the offer. On hearing her expectations, you are surprised to know that this is more than what the US office told you. You were told that the ratio of the salary between the US and India should be in the range of 1:5 to 1:4, but here you are finding it somewhat skewed. You will have to ask again for the increase in the budget. You have done a good exercise last year on all these aspects but things have changed since then. You worry that one of the important reasons of opening the offshore, which is to cut costs is getting defeated. Even the service companies are offering a better deal with fewer overheads.

What will you do?

Case 4.3: One of the sectors in the US multinational is lagging in the market place, as it does not have the required features in its product to take on the competitor. In their discussion, the CEO suggests to the VP of that division that other divisions are utilizing the skills in India well and advises him to look into expanding the India operations by executing projects from this sector too.

The VP discusses this with his staff and they come up with a plan to form a parallel release team (one in US and one in India), so that features can be released on a six-month rather than yearly basis, which is happening currently. One of the directors comes to India and leverages the infrastructure of the other division. Her mandate is to hire ten senior technical people in two months and bring them to the US for product understanding. Later on in the next six months, a team of fifty people will be hired and trained by the initial team. The actual work on the new release should begin starting on the seventh month. She does her best in short listing, interviewing, convincing and getting the proper approval from the US to hire this initial team. After two months, she manages to hire only five people. She feels that these five are good and some of them are very good and resisted the pressure of hiring more by lowering the bar. She sends these five people to US and continues looking for more candidates.

As the hiring plan is slipping, the VP changes the direction for the India team. He decides together with his staff, that until they reach critical mass in India, they will not start working on a parallel team. However, the hiring that was completed in India should be utilized in helping the US team to achieve the right quality in this release itself and later on, they will reconsider the parallel release plan. This change in plan de-motivates the engineers from India, currently in the US. They send their resignation letters to her in India and ask her to help them in returning to India at the earliest, as helping the existing team does not require much design and architecture challenges for which they have joined the project.

She panics as this will not only hinder the overall plan but also spread the word in the industry, which will make hiring more difficult.

How can you help her?

Case 4.4: One of the engineers sends his resignation letter to his manager and requests for an early relieving date. As per the company policy, a person is supposed to give two months of notice before leaving the company. The manager is shocked to receive this email, as he is one of the high performers and there was no prior sign of any dissatisfaction in any of the previous dialogs. He handles a critical module and though there is another person, who knows some parts of that module, but his exit will still have a major impact.

The manager discusses with him and he mentions that he just wants to move forward. He says that he is satisfied with the work challenge, salary and other benefits and the new job is somewhat a lateral move and nothing more.

On probing further, the engineer reveals that he is concerned with the retrenchment or toned down scope of his work as the company has not been doing well for multiple quarters and the share prices are steadily dropping. The company where he is joining is a young company and he can contribute in some non-engineering activities too that can help him in the future. The domain of work is the same.

The manager initially tries to convince him. He communicates to the Senior Director, who is located at the headquarters to talk to this engineer on the phone. The Senior Director clarifies most of his doubts and shares the product roadmap, market strategy and the path to regain market leadership. The engineer appears to be convinced. At which the Senior Director even offers him to come to the headquarters and spend time to learn more.

After the call, the Senior Director informs the manager that there is some news here that one of our competitors is opening up an Indian offshore center and therefore he suspects that they might start poaching some key resources from here and it looks like this person could be joining that company. He warns the manager to come up with a plan at the earliest before others follow the same path.

If you are the manager, what will you do?

5 Culture & Policies

A company is known by the culture it keeps. This is the DNA of any company. People speak on company culture years after they have left. Hence, the right culture provides a sense of pride to the employees within and outside the workplace.

Though we live in a global village, country specific culture still plays a major role. The culture of a global company has two major contributing factors: one is the culture based on the location of the headquarters of the company, second is the local culture. There are variations in the culture based on whether they are in the east coast of the US, west coast of the US, Europe, Japan, Korea, China, and the Gulf. Mr. Terrance Brake's "The Global Leader"[9] covers this topic very well.

The work force in India has worked closely with US-based companies for almost three decades and European companies (particularly, British) for a century in the traditional manufacturing, mining and service sectors. Therefore, there is a fair understanding amongst them. In the last decade, when some East Asian companies

9. The Global Leader, Terence Brake, Irwin Professional Publishing, 1997

started their operations in India, there were many surprises and culture shocks experienced by both sides. It has taken time to understand and appreciate the cultures and come to a common ground. Now, people can change jobs with more ease, regardless of the culture of the parent company.

So what is special about the culture of the Indian IT industry? This is a very sensitive subject to write about, as anything written on this topic will generate plenty of criticism. It is also a gross injustice in skipping out many more aspects of Indian culture. Hence, it is best to mention a few idiosyncrasies unique to the culture and the perspective parent companies should take.

"Compare and Contrast" Culture

Indian people train children to value academic and scholastic achievements. The competitive comparison in schools and colleges carries through to the workplace, comparing salaries and performance ratings at work. This is not limited to individuals; even parents discuss their kids' achievements in their social circles, which can include details of compensation benefits and rewards.

Ultimately, this becomes a vicious circle, which can easily lead to dissatisfaction if taken beyond healthy competition. This occurrence has decreased somewhat in the last decade due to the understanding of people with more experience. However, it is still prevalent at the entry level.

This practice is not restricted within the company, but also discussed with friends across companies. They have complete knowledge of benefits and compensation that a particular company provides.

Even though they share it outside, they are sensitive to keep the company's confidential matters within company grounds. This freely available information does have one aspect; it provides current competitive salary compensation that can help in recruitment and retention.

"Social" Culture

People do not join the company as just another place of employment, but they join it for work combined with social environment. The expectations of their supervisors extend to and include fulfilling the role of a senior family member (more prevalent at junior levels). Here they might share their personal issues. In this case, it is important to work out a win-win proposition for the employee by considering their personal circumstances, as much as possible. In extreme cases, one might have to provide a reference of good conduct to a prospective father-in-law of the employee.

People are sensitive to criticism especially with respect to their work output. If you have to provide tough messages, most prefer it "sugar coated", but the manager should not hesitate in providing a blunt one if the situation warrants.

As they form a social circle, it is difficult to get feedback on an employee's peers. They often address the issue in an ambiguous way, as the person will think it might affect their friendship. The positive aspect to this is an increase in teamwork. They might work together for extra hours on weekdays or come on weekends to work in addition to their social outings.

"Seniority" Culture

In Indian society, age and knowledge are important factors in commanding respect. Age usually takes precedence over knowledge. This is a concept, which no doubt bleeds into the workplace. Even though it is a performance-based system, it is not as prevalent as it is in the West. Unlike the US, where you can find a 33-year old VP, in India this trend has only recently started and is taking time to set-in completely. Normally for the first 5-10 years of one's career, the difference will not be drastic between the average performer and the top-notch performer. By that time, the person is already in his early 30s. However, after that, the differences based on performance will become apparent. Around this time a career crisis begins to take affect (for more detail, please refer to the chapter on people management).

At this point, they may also start realizing that every organization has a pyramid structure. Some work hard to get it right, some take time to rectify it and some never learn.

Unlike in the West, where a manager has experiences of providing higher salary to his employee compared to himself, this rarely happens in India. If this does occur, it either is corrected, or remains painful to digest. This can be due to one of two circumstances: First, a senior technical person may earn more but for administrative purposes reports to a manager in his own salary band but with a lower salary. Second, the person might be younger than the manager and be in the lower salary band, but receive high ratings year after year and might be at the high end of his salary range, which would be higher than the low positioning of the manager's salary in his band.

There are few such cases, but its prevalence should begin to take shape as India strengthens its technical ladder. Many companies have introduced a technical ladder within the last decade, but this will take time to develop completely.

This seniority feeling does not stop within a company. People may not join another company if the new designation appears to be of a lower social status than the current designation, in spite of higher responsibility and increased salary.

Layoffs at the senior level have started happening in India too and slowly like in the West, people have started realizing that today's VP can be a manager tomorrow.

"Difficult to Say No" Culture

One needs to understand the meaning of "no" to someone from a culture, where "no" does not mean just "no". Saying "no" can have various connotations: It can mean that the person is impolite. It can also be that the person is disobeying. Sometimes people interpret it, as a mark or a dent in a good working relationship. The above-mentioned ones are the external perspective. On the other hand, a person can think that if he says "No", the manager will feel that he has lesser skills or that he will not take the challenge as it might influence the appraisal.

The side impact is that sometimes, when one hears "no" at such a late stage in a project it becomes difficult to save it. It also creates a ripple effect in the project.

On the upside, a person who wants to take it as a challenge will learn fast and make things happen. He will put extra effort to get it done. Therefore, the fundamental issue is clear communication. Some of them are good at stating so upfront, but most of them are still learning to say it candidly.

It is better to ask very clearly and make sure that they understand that there is no harm in saying "no". It is important to set a culture where the following ingredients are present:

- Invite/encourage/expect that bad news should be stated early

- Never shoot the messenger

- Provide many opportunities in group settings and in 1on1 settings

- Ask for bad news, risk items (including potential)

- Responsibility on the individual to identify the risk

Trust

The company that is being setup or is operational will not be successful if the core ingredients of trust are not present between the parent organization and the India operations.

Trust is mutual and plays a significant (but hidden) role in the success an Indian office. It is true that building trust does not happen overnight. It is also true that building the long bridge of mutual trust and respect gradually happens through each interaction. Achieving this requires significant effort and energy because both parties need to provide transparency in their dealings, with a mix of delegation and control. It is the duty of the parent organization to take the first steps towards building and maintaining trust.

Here are some examples of issues that can lead to mistrust if not handled properly:

A VP finance of the parent company starts working with the newly formed management team in India. They jointly decide that accounting and payroll should be outsourced and one person from the Indian team should coordinate the activities. So far, the intention is good. Slowly, the outsourced company starts having direct interaction with the VP finance without keeping the India employee in the loop. This leads to an environment wherein the outsourced company double-checks the suggestions from the India employee rather than the other way round. One can easily avoid this situation by empowering the India office in decision making and extracting the right output from the outsourced company. In addition, the VP finance can setup proper process of reporting financial transactions from India and can do some audits to receive extra assurance about the compliance.

The parent company hires a law firm in India based on recommendations received through its own contacts. This is fine even without consulting the Indian management team, because corporate level decisions take precedence over keeping everyone in the loop. It might happen that the legal firm in the parent company has relations with the firm in India or may have a better understanding with this particular firm in India. This can help in resolving the issues amicably at the global level. An issue may arise when the parent company starts relying more on the legal firm compared to the India head. The legal firm will have final say on contract negotiations with the third party, it will have the authority to sign higher value vouchers. The parent company is not using the legal firm as a consultant but using them as a tool to run the India operation indirectly. This leads to a situation where the India head will start focusing more on engineering and will leave all non-engineering decisions on parent company and the legal firm. This will lead to making decisions in isolation and without taking the engineering inputs, causing resentment in the employees. A better way to handle this is by making the role and responsibility of the India head clear and by ensuring proper documentation of the approval process of non-engineering activities.

The head of the Indian operation is in good tandem with the parent company. The parent company begins talks on merger and acquisition. This leads to a reduction in the frequency of conference calls with India due to a lack of available time. The parent company transfers a good amount of funds well in advance for running the operation smoothly. Within a short time, another request for a fund transfer comes, which is honored. After a couple of months during the audit, the miscellaneous expenses reveal that the India head has spent a large amount of money in tools without approval from the parent company. Moreover, those tools were not in line with the company effort to standardize the tools across all locations. The weekly report does not mention it and the parent company did not examine the expense reports in detail at the time. A couple of lessons abound from this example. Proper documentation of the approval process is important. This should have two aspects: Multiple levels of approval based on amount of purchase and the requirement to take an approval in case the fund is used other than for the actual approved items. In addition to this, the finance person should be on dotted lines with the parent company (if it is not a shared service).

An Engineering manager in India executes the project as indicated by the agreed plan and provides the results to the responsible manager in the parent company. The data, provided to the parent company, is shared with a prospective customer. The customer makes some enquiries and seeks clarifications. In the detailed interaction with the engineering manager, the data reveals that some information is extrapolated rather than actually generated. Since the report does not mention this clearly, it leads to a misunderstanding between the manager of the parent company and the customer. The manager at the parent company has to apologize to the customer. To avoid these types of issues easily, one needs to ask the right questions, be on top of activities and be in contact frequently. These steps will help in finding out assumptions, which might not be of significance to one team, but could be important for another.

A person at the parent company, who has joined recently after replacing the existing manager, is responsible for one of the projects executed in India. He has good relations with a service company in collaboration with which he has executed a project with his previous organization. He decides to shift the existing project from India to that company and provides a new project to the team in India. Once the transition is over, he requests for the quality metrics of the existing software from the service company. On receiving the data, he directly asks the manager at the India office for an explanation on some of the metrics. The manager in India would have to dig up all the old charts and the risks communicated with the parent company. In addition, he has to provide the decision and the background of the decision. The manager in India gets frustrated, feels distrusted and thinks his skills are coming into question. This is a delicate issue and the supervisor who might have a genuine reason in asking the historical data should handle it properly. He should do this by setting the right perspective and making the purpose of his request explicitly clear.

All the above scenarios are manageable, as it requires careful planning and good, frequent communication. It is better to start with trust in the case of new relationships, until an incidence causes doubt and further consequences convert doubt into certainty.

Now let us look into the scenarios, which might be fine in the West, but can become a trust issue in India.

It is common to have "skip level" (In formal settings, manager's manager talking with the manager's subordinate in the absence of manager) dialog in the West. In India, this is not common. It takes time to setup this type of culture as the manager might feel that they are not being trusted and are being double-checked by talking to his team members directly. The purpose of this type of dialog is not to find fault in the manager, but to get the pulse of the team and to act fast if something appears serious. The issue can be on work content, work environment, company policy or any other serious issues. A manager's manager can provide input to the manager on handling some of the issues in his own team. He can also provide early warnings on a potential people issue and equip the manager in handling it soon. Once the manager starts to see the benefit in this, his support for the process will begin to take shape. The success of this dialog lies in the skill of the manager's manager, but can be disastrous if not executed properly.

In the West, it is normal for commitments to be based on business needs, but in India, it is taken as a promise. Therefore, one should be very careful in communicating and putting the proper caveat to it. For example, any overseas travel and the duration of stay communicated to an employee will become binding, and any changes to this bond will cause a loss of trust. It is important to explain in the beginning that business needs are paramount in fulfilling such commitments. Similarly, clearly explain any change in work assignment and other work-related issues.

One needs to be sensitive in handling the issues of average or low performers who have worked in the company for a long time and who have contributed well in the past, but now have entered into a comfort zone and contribute far less than expected. Motivate them by counseling, moving them to other teams or providing them another role in the same team. If everything fails and the management asks a team member to leave, then explain the reasons for this carefully. In such a case, the person would have built a good network of his own and he might portray himself as a victim of the "use and throw" philosophy of management. Therefore, it is important that people themselves realize and agree with management that the contribution is below average in spite of various opportunities provided to them.

Productivity Data

This is one major source of having a feeling of mistrust in India. Some of the common productivity questions are, "how many lines of code are written per day per engineer?", "how many manual test cases executed per day per engineer?", "how many test cases automated per day per engineer?", "how many bugs are found against per KLOC (Kilo Lines of Code)?" The parent company should lead by example and follow standard practices that are enforce across all locations to collect and publish the productivity data. There should not be an underlying sentiment of: It is often asked by the Indian team and not from other teams. In extreme cases, it is also used to justify whether it is still wise to get the project done in India (by comparing this data against the per engineer cost data). These exercises, if done before giving any work to India are fine, but during the execution process and making them, applicable only to the India team causes discouragement and low morale.

Feeling of Secondary Citizen

Even though not stated overtly, the style of interaction, the choice of words and the level of expectation communicates the intent of the management team of the parent company towards the teams in India. One can easily make it out in which project team members in India are feeling empowered and in which they are not. It will be in the interest of the parent company to extend the treatment of equality in order to get higher output from the same team. In addition, it is important for the India team to rise to the occasion and grab the opportunity. If they continue to work on "tell" mode, (i.e. let the parent company tell me what we have to do and we will just do that) then they will continue being below par in the content of their work and in their contribution to the overall success of the company.

As organizations are becoming flatter and matrix-driven, it is possible to have a solid or dotted line reporting across geography in either direction depending upon specific functions or roles or projects. One rarely sees a team in the parent organization reporting to an India manager. Therefore, it is important to have the focus on logical teaming for better results, rather than purely based on geography.

Teamwork

The whole concept of teamwork came from rewarding result-oriented performance. A formation of a core team occurs when the company shifts a bulk of employees from a certain company or hires them based on referrals from existing employees. This helps in teamwork, but can lead to a couple of issues. The company will have an imported culture of the other company from where most of the people were hired. In such a situation, the group positions itself as the primary citizen and owns all critical activities, while future employees automatically become secondary citizens, performing peripheral work. This is because they trust the existing ones more than they trust newcomers. If the employer kept this perspective in mind during hiring, then it is fine, otherwise, this will not be good from the teaming and retention perspective. People have often left the company feeling that management does not trust new employees and hence does not give them full responsibility. It should be the challenge of the management team not to fall into this trap and ensure a smooth induction of all employees in a seamless way, so that people do not feel secondary.

Once an employee joins and becomes a part of the family, it is in the interest of all to bring the person up to speed quickly, and make sure that they enjoy the trust and faith of all. Senior employees continue to enjoy a better grasp on the product, the history of changes done in the product, and many experiences and decisions taken at different times. It is important to assign the right job to the right person based on their capabilities, rather than the employee identification number.

Openness and Transparency

One has to setup and continuously reinforce an open and transparent environment where information flows freely. Information should always be available to the individual who needs it. This environment will help people feel free to share their thoughts, provide suggestions for improvement and, most importantly, give and receive direct feedback.

This also helps in reducing rumors and ensures that people spend more time and energy on their work rather than worrying about things they want to know and do not have information about.

Having Fun

No work environment can be successful without having some recreational activities. Some office facilities do provide recreational activities. One can have a wide variety of activities at the company or team level. These activities can be for the employees and sometimes for their families too. One should avoid arranging boring parties done for the sake of having one. These parties are monotonous and marked with long speeches followed by dinner or lunch, which leave no room for people to interact and strengthen their team spirits.

Parties should have some team building exercises too. The fundamental benefit that one receives is to interact well with other team members providing an opportunity to smoothen the relationships, which might have strained during the heat of product development. Both employees and their families remember a good party. Attendance in these parties will also increase. Occasionally, the employees can also go out for an afternoon or late evening event in small teams. It is also advisable to avoid any award ceremony at events where family is present, as it will be difficult to answer one's kid or spouse on why he or she did not get the award while a few others did.

Institution Building

The intention to build an institution should be there from day one. A culture that is setup for a small team needs to withstand the test of time, when the team size grows year after year. Similarly, formulating and setting up the company policies is important because once the organization is big, it should retain its original allowing for only a few changes as it grows.

In terms of policies, it is important that policies should be set keeping the various government regulations in mind. A legal team should review policies thoroughly in order to ensure that one is compliant. A good knowledge is required of generally acceptable practices prevalent in the industry.

The first step towards setting up policy is to publish an employee handbook with a clear set of guidelines. Establish policies and practices in the very beginning, so that everyone can apply a uniform set of policies. This will avoid making decisions on a case-by-case basis.

Generally, management does not pay attention to this when the company is small. Everyone knows each other and they enjoy flexibility in having individual-based decisions, "one-off" type of waivers, situational incentives and many tactical or on the spot decisions. As the company starts growing, some of them will quote precedence; some will get situational benefits and some will not. This will poison the teamwork, as there will be haves and have-nots. There will even be disparity on the level of benefits enjoyed by many. The "compare and contrast" culture will come into picture, resulting in lack of happiness in the whole organization. This situation will trigger an employee handbook. Now, employees will complain about benefits, which they used to enjoy, but now withdrawn. As a result, employees will feel that the company does not care for them. Balancing employee's expectations together with forceful but fair implementation of policies will become a Herculean task.

The management needs to ensure that managerial discretions should be an exception, rather than a practice. This helps in spreading the feeling of fairness in implementing the policies and practices.

Please see Appendix C for important policies required. It is important to put the right focus on policies, as it has much more India centric practices, which might be new to many in parent organizations.

Compensation Philosophy

This differs from company to company. It consists of two components:

Salary & Stock Options: It is better to have a philosophy statement and to review it annually. Implementing this for a global organization is possible in many ways. Two commonly used options are:

Option 1: Some companies follow the same positioning world-wide. For example,

Salary: Will be positioned at 75th percentile in India compared to the India market and the 75th percentile in the US compared to the US market.

Stock: Normally, employees receive the same amount of stock in the same band or level or grade irrespective of the location. For example a person in engineering grade 7, will receive 500 stock whether in the US or India.

Option 2: On local market conditions, some companies place salary at a higher percentile specifically in countries where the job market is hot. For example:

Salary: The Company might position the India team at 90th percentile in comparison with the India industry, while positioned at 70th percentile in the US in comparison with the US industry.

Stock Options: Normally they lower the stock options where the salary is at higher percentile. For example, a person in engineering grade 7 will receive 500 stock options in the US, and the employee in the same grade in India will receive 400 stock options.

Lack of a compensation philosophy will lead to issues not only for the people who move from one geographical location to another in the same company but also erode confidence in regards to fairness.

Performance Appraisal

It is a good practice to apply the same performance appraisal policy across all locations. The Indian office should have the same yardstick used in ranking and distribution. Many companies do a 360-degree feedback session at the end of the appraisal cycle. In addition to it, one should provide and receive feedback at regular intervals of 3-4 times a year. People do appreciate receiving feedback with specific examples. If there is some important feedback, then one should give it immediately rather than waiting for a future date when dialog is scheduled. Realize that people always welcome honest and candid feedback.

Salary Revision

Many companies acquire a salary survey against the set of companies with whom they would like to get the information. These are collected against various bands linked with roles and responsibilities. However, some of these bands may not be applicable to the organization. The company also determines its compensation philosophy of positioning the organization at a certain percentile. Once the company performs these two activities and develops a new salary range on per-band-basis, then the employees receive a new salary range based on their performance. Some organizations use the base salary and provide percentages for hikes, while a few companies set the target salary range, irrespective of the existing salary.

For example, a company states the new salary band should be between USD 24K to USD 26K. A person is getting USD 20K and the company determines that the overall raise will be in the range 13-18% for the particular band. In this case, in spite of giving an 18% raise, they will not be able to come to the target range. Therefore, a few companies do away with percentage increase and pull the people to the new band in spite of their existing salary. This also helps in people management where a historically low salary is discontinued as a base salary year after year.

In a job market, companies may give semi-annual salary hikes. Some of the companies have separate cycles for delivering salary raises and stocks grants, making employees feel rewarded frequently.

Culture & Policies Summarized:

One needs to take time in carefully drafting the policies to make sure that every word has clear meaning. This will help in removing any misinterpretation. Policies should not be set to solve the problem at hand, or with the attitude that this will be good for now. The policies should be set, keeping in mind that one is building an institution and that longevity and stability are key. To create an atmosphere of fair treatment, implement immunity to the policy only in exceptional cases.

Culture & Policy Case Studies:

Case 5.1: One manager has a team of fifteen engineers and he reports to the US office. His team structure is the following:

Engineers: four

Senior Engineers: eight

Lead Engineers: three

All the four people in Engineers band have two years of experience and have a similar educational background.

At the time of appraisal, the manager follows the process of collecting feedback from various people within and outside the team and he fits his team based on the Bell curve model specified by the HR.

The following rating is given (A: being highest and E: being lowest):

Engineer-1: A: Recommended for promotion to Senior Engineer

Engineer-2: B

Engineer-3: C

Engineer-4: C

During the normalization process with his peers and US based supervisor, the manager presents his case well and walks out of the meeting without any change.

After the rating, the manager decides on a salary hike. He follows the HR guideline by sticking to the range for the hike and the total budget allocated. The manager places Engineer-1 in the middle of the range, which is an acceptable decision for the hike. He will get an additional hike that comes out from "promotion" budget. Engineer-2 is already at the high end of the band and therefore gets only the normal hike. The manager knows that Engineer-3 is somewhat a complainer of sorts, and he tries to be sensitive by providing him the best possible hike for his rating. Since Engineer-4 ranks lowest in his band, the manager pulls him to match Engineer-3's final salary and therefore giving Engineer-4 a significant percentage hike.

The Manager is satisfied that he has completed this activity. He then starts the appraisal dialog. Here are the comments from the engineers during the appraisal dialog.

Engineer-1: *"I am very happy with the recognition and the promotion you have given to me. Thanks a lot."*

Engineer-2: *"I am happy with the ratings and I have no comments."*

Engineer-3: *" I was expecting a higher rating as we all have worked very hard, also I came to know that you have promoted one of us to the next level. I am not convinced that I am judged correctly and this is de-motivating me."*

Engineer-4: *"I have shown flexibility and worked on all assignments. You have changed my work content too and I delivered that too, yet you have rated me average, which is somewhat disturbing. You have given a higher rating to a few others in my own project team where both our contributions are the same."*

After a week or so, the manager hands the hike letter. Here are the comments from Engineers.

Engineer-1: *"I was so happy with the promotion but I was expecting a better hike, as was given to my friend in another team. The hike looks somewhat disproportionate with the rating."*

Engineer-2: "*After the dialog I came to know that you promoted one of my project team members. I fail to understand why I was not promoted. This hike appears to be bogus. Have I done anything wrong?*"

Engineer-3: "*I have already communicated my dissatisfaction to you during the dialog and this hike is adding further to my woes. It looks like that I have got the lowest in my friend circle.*"

Engineer-4: "*It is good that this hike has corrected the past mistake, but still the average rating is bothering me.*"

Therefore, all four engineers have shown dissatisfaction in the end either on rating or on hike or on both. The manager feels miserable and discusses with his supervisor who is sitting in the US office. The Supervisor is puzzled on how this information leaked and advises the HR to tighten the process for better confidentiality. Now he slowly starts understanding the "compare and contrast culture".

What should the manager do?

Case 5.2: A Europe based company opens an India development center and wants to shift a product to India for further development and maintenance. This product has a good installed base and receives new feature requests, change requests and issues from its customers. Susan, a senior manager will work with an Indian counterpart in forming the team and getting them trained in the technology, product and process. She takes it up as a challenge and ensures that the initial team members travel to Europe to familiarize with the company. She takes extra effort in making sure that some of them can visit the customer location to appreciate the way the product is used. Whenever the parent company distributes any T-Shirts or any goodies, she gets them ordered for the India team too, and sends it across India for distribution. She has won the hearts of many of the engineers and they feel friendly talking to her. Bhaskar, a senior manager in India is working around the clock getting his team trained in-house and has begun work on their travel arrangements so that they can go to Europe. He has also earned the respect from his team. Both of the managers work hand in hand in making sure that this team can ramp-up fast. The first 3 to 4 months go well; the team size grows to around 30 with three teams (two development teams and one test team) and each headed by a manager, who reports to Bhaskar.

The work on the first release starts after the India technical core team returns from the Europe office where they have acquired a proper understanding of the work. Susan is surprised to find that some of the activities are over estimated and some of them under estimated. She does not have in-depth technical knowledge and hence she calls one of the technical associates in India to understand this estimation.

He explains, "This schedule is made by managers. We have provided the effort estimation, and have divided the features into three-risk categories i.e. high, medium and low based on effort estimation and the confidence on understanding the impacted areas in the code to implement the features. It would be better if you can talk to the manager, as they will have a better perspective of the full program."

She requests, "This is great that you categorized them in various buckets. Can you send me the sheet that you have sent to your manager?"

The engineer sends her the sheet and copies his manager.

The manager immediately escalates the issue to Bhaskar. Bhaskar sends her an email and states that it would be better if she could direct her questions to him rather than asking the engineer who might not have a full picture.

She replies that he is reading too much, into her asking the engineer questions. She says that in a transparent organization, information sharing is a healthy sign.

After a while, she receives a project plan from Bhaskar. She calls Bhaskar and suggests him to pull the date by a month, as this is too late.

Bhaskar replies that this is the best schedule and he cannot accommodate any change without de-prioritizing the feature.

This upsets her; she calls one of the managers and suggests that he ask his team members to come in on weekends for a month with proper compensation for their effort.

He immediately reports this to Bhaskar. Bhaskar becomes furious, responding that one month of working during the weekends is insufficient since performing these additional activities require a couple of months and one needs to line up other teams too. He says that many of them have put in for vacation in October(due to religious festival) and he does not want to cancel their vacations, as it will not help unless few features are dropped..

Bhaskar copies his manager in this email.

She is shocked to see the issue escalated to senior management in India, though she was just trying to explore some options.

She decides to come to India.

Bhaskar tells his manager "I am fed up with her. She interferes a lot. If she is not getting information on time, or if she is getting incorrect information then she can ask you. Nevertheless, she does not trust me and has a bad habit of cross checking each email of mine with my juniors. She should just specify the requirements and monitor the major milestone, but she has begun to micromanage the engineers. Only recently, she was telling me that Anish is feeling de-motivated and that I should do some job rotation. I feel like telling my team, not to provide any information to her without my knowledge"

Susan comes to India office and goes to meet Bhaskar's boss.

She responds, "What is wrong with Bhaskar? Initially, he was so cooperative and supportive, but off late, he has become very irritable. He expects me not to talk to anyone. This is a transparent organization, why can't I talk with them? He should understand the type of help and support I provide from the headquarters. If I do not have full information then I will not be able to answer the questions that management keeps asking me. I have to shield the whole India team and help engineers when they come here. If they confide their feelings and issues with me and not with their managers then who is at fault. If Bhaskar can be open and share with me all the efforts which he has done to come to this decision then I can communicate the same to my management with confidence."

Say you are Bhaskar's manager, what would you suggest?

6 People Management

The Indian IT industry is marked for their heavy dependence on people—this is their largest resource, and hence people management is of paramount importance.

People are central to the organization. Because of this, any good manager needs to spend a significant amount of time in people management. Stephen P Robbins and Mary Coutler, authors of "Management"[10] say that the time spent in human skills remain more or less the same for all levels of management.

It should be a constant endeavor of the manager to ensure that individual aspirations and organizational goals always align. This helps in minimizing people issues and streamlining effort to achieve the company goals. Some issues can be major and require intense discussions and convincing, while some minor issues only need simple solutions. Whatever the issue may be, if not resolved amicably, it can create dissatisfaction and de-motivation. Sometimes, the issue cannot be resolved at all, and in this case, it might be best if both parties' separated.

---

10. Management, Stephen P Robbins and Mary Coutler,
    Prentice Hall, Upper Saddle Rive, New Jersey 07458, 1996

Nevertheless, a serious and sincere effort is required from management on every issue as people do appreciate and reciprocate effort and honesty of the management.

No organization can keep all employees happy all the time, but one needs to try to keep the percentage of happy employees high. The best way to tackle any people issue is to deal with the problem directly. Listen keenly to the issue and try to deal with it in full honesty and sincerity, or be direct in telling the employee that resolving the issue is simply not doable. Leaving it open within the promised timeline will further aggravate the issue. However bitter the truth is, one should always be willing to confront it. By being proactive, discussing, listening, and interacting with employees, one must inform the employees early in regards to any issue. This can help in examining whether the issue is prevalent at an individual level, team level or even at a wider level. Individual issues are best handled by dialog, while team and organization issues are better resolved through all-hands meetings, mass email, or through multiple small team meetings. In some cases, it might also involve modifying policies and procedures at the organization level.

Coaching and mentoring are the tools that any manager should use efficiently. In this fast-changing work environment, issues can be resolved by providing adequate time in patiently listening to them. This also helps in improving productivity.

As this is a knowledge-intensive industry, people issues are somewhat different from the other traditional industries. People issues can arise due to any of the following:

Career Crisis

A crisis in career can happen to anyone at any time. The Random House dictionary defines career as a "Progress or general course of action of a person through life or through some phase of life." There will always be vicissitudes in one's career.

Here are Three Examples to Elaborate:

A reputed company hires a person, where he had everything on his side—position, compensation, recognition and so on. He joins the new company to provide technical leadership to a small team. After a month or so, it becomes clear that he does not have sufficient in-depth skills to perform his job. In his previous job, he was simply maintaining a mature product that did not provide him with enough challenges, leading to his skills rusting. Management suggests he relinquish his current role for the time being, and acquire the appropriate skills. He finds this humiliating and decides to quit.

In another instance, there is a senior person who has received very high ratings in the past. The management ignored him for higher roles on a couple of occasions and he received no proper feedback from his manager about improving his performance. In a sudden restructuring, he begins reporting to a different manager. As a veteran in the company, he easily predicts every task. He is in a comfort zone and does not see any need to improve his skill sets. The new manager observes him for six months and gives him feedback stating that he has spent too much time with the company, and that it would be better for him to take up new challenges in a new environment. The new environment will not be predictable and therefore would be full of excitement that would trigger an urge for him to improve. The senior was surprised that after investing his prime years in the organization and giving it his best, he was now being asked to leave. In the end, the person resigned from the company, after issuing a statement that "if the manager's suggestion worked he would be thankful, otherwise he would feel victimized." After three months, the senior called the manager to thank him.

One other person, quite junior in experience but with an accomplished educational background, is assigned to the system software development activities in her first job. During the first year, she received an average rating, while on her second year, she received a below average rating. She was adamant that she had the required skills and possessed the right educational background; therefore, she could not be below average. The case escalated to the second level of management. In multiple discussions, the management discovered that the person was unable to concentrate on any one activity for long time, but did well when she handled multiple activities of less intense depth. Based on this discovery, the management transferred her to a customer support role, where such skills are required and she began to excel in her new position.

The Bottom Line Is: management should know an employee's strengths and weaknesses in order to utilize them in a most efficient capacity. The effort required to go a notch above in one's strength is far less than the effort required in improving a weakness by a notch. It is advisable to read, "Now Discover your Strengths" by Marcus Buckingham and Donald Clifton[11], who captures this topic very well.

Some people know their strengths and weaknesses very well, but try to experiment with the job/activity in an area in which they do not have much previous experience or success. This is fine as it will provide a new outlook, but they need to be prepared to spend time to be successful and even then, it might not yield the desired results.

There have been cases where a person may have many years of experience, but they have not stayed on for more than one or two years at any project or job. This person has obviously not developed the breadth and depth required to handle the full life cycle of a project. Many people face similar career issues from having made wrong choices: following a technical ladder instead of the management ladder, development versus support, development versus testing and so on. They do not explore other career options, such as build or configuration management, technical writing, product support, product management, or system engineering functions.

Sometime the crisis happens when people want to take up a higher responsibility prematurely. The company may even encourage this because they are a star performer in their current role, without considering that the star performer in the current role does not automatically make them eligible for the other role where the required skill set is different.

---

11. Now, Discover Your Strenghts, Marcus Buckingham & Donald Clifton, The free press, 2001

It is also important to define the technical ladder and make it attractive. This way, people who are suitable for the technical ladder will not clutter the management ladder due to its non-availability or unattractiveness. One should define the role and responsibility clearly, so that the technical ladder is not just an advisory function but also that the individuals who are a part of the ladder are held accountable and responsible for their decisions and suggestions.

A serious situation occurs when a person is not aware of skills that have become outdated and does not accept feedback.

Appraisal Process

The appraisal process in most organizations is an annual affair. Many companies follow the process of receiving a 360-degree feedback on an individual, and decide ratings based on such a multi-dimensional feedback. There are plenty of people who do not agree with these ratings--especially if they are rated with "meets expectation", or "on plan", or "Average".

Few high performers will be unhappy if they receive feedback such as "very good" as opposed to "exceptional". A leader should have frequent dialogs with their employees and maintain a record of such conversations. People like to hear examples and for this reason, managers should do homework very thoroughly before giving an appraisal—whether minor or major.

If an issue is serious enough, it is important to provide feedback instantaneously rather than waiting for an annual review. People do appreciate direct feedback. It is normal for people to mention other names and compare their ratings. It is important that managers be well prepared to ensure that they can differentiate each person's contribution clearly within the team. In addition, it is important that managers should retain and send out a clear picture when a team is working on a single issue. Different ratings for each member of the team will lead to doubts, anxiety, and heartburn. Therefore, it is important to establish a clear distinction of work and a proper tracking system within a team.

Negative feedback practices could aggravate the situation. For example, statements like "I wanted to give you a higher rating, but my supervisor disagrees," or "I have a quota and that's why I cannot accommodate you," or worse, "I will take care of you next time," are potential building blocks for disaster. Managers should be mastered in delivering proper feedback that will take employees to a higher rating, rather than showing helplessness or delivering false promises in their statements. If the employee is still not satisfied, then managers should feel confident to escalate the dialogue to a higher level.

The most difficult situations are with the low performers. Leaders should spend a considerable amount of time in these cases, since the person will rarely agree that he or she has performed below expectations. If the manager has periodically provided candid feedback to the person, the rating should not come as a surprise. If all other means of improvements have been tried and failed, it may be best to ask them to look for other employment.

Pay Hike

This is another major cause for people issues. In order to avoid confusion, it is important to explain the compensation package and the awards process clearly. Normally, various parameters determine a salary: the market data at various bands, the company's decision to position itself at a particular percentile inside the band, the person's current performance rating and current salary. Performance rating normally gets more weight in salary revision.

Each employee will surely have some inclination of his or her market value through his or her friends in other companies and colleagues in the same company. These few data points set the expectation. If the hike is at par or above their expectation, they will be satisfied, but if it is below what they expect, frustration will set in. The compensation team should be extremely careful, be well attuned to the market value of each employee and deliver a granular performance rating that will justify the hikes awarded to each employee.

In a hot market, some organizations give out midterm hikes. If one places the salary at a higher percentile with reference to companies working on a similar domain, an annual review is standard. However, if the company positions salaries inadequately, then it will require mid term or frequent salary corrections.

Designation & Promotion

Traditionally, Indian industries have hierarchical organizational setups. Some companies have more than ten levels and some divide these levels into multiple sublevels. Each level and sublevel should have designations. This provides the company with the ability to move people to the next level/sub-level every two or three years based on performance, giving employees a feeling of moving up the ladder.

This is also true with other large MNCs. After the bubble bursts, many MNCs start moving towards a flat organization, and hence start cutting down the number of levels to less than ten. A few India offices have followed the global guideline strictly, but some have added an Indian flavor, providing some intermediate levels too.

The service industry propels the growth of the Indian IT industry. The service industry has its own organizational models and multiple designations geared towards their business models. The number of people in the organization also marks its growth.

All These Combined Pose Multiple People Issues:

Some people would not like to join an organization if the perceived image of the offered designation in the new company is lower than their designation at the existing company, despite a higher salary, a better role, and well-defined responsibility. These are label-conscious people.

There are widely used designations in India like "module lead", "technical lead", "project lead", which are either non-existent abroad or have different meanings. This is also the case with designations like "system analyst", "architect", and "staff engineer."

For example, the designation of "architect" comes early in the service industry, but in product companies, these designations come late in the career. In addition, the responsibility of the "architect" will also vary between product companies. It is important to clarify the role and responsibility upfront to avoid misconceptions.

People prefer designations that they can profess to be in, especially within their social circle of friends from different IT companies. Some people would like a higher designation for other reasons too: fetching better responses on marriage proposals, or getting a better deal from banks on loans.

Similarly, people in product companies might face an issue vis-à-vis the service industry, as the growth is more in the technical expertise, rather than the number of people managed.

The sense of upward movement every two years—especially based on designation—will be an issue in a flat organization. It is the manager's responsibility in enhancing the content of the employee's role. This way, the person will not feel outdated compared to his peers in other companies, something that will help him in retaining his competitive edge in spite of not being in a higher designation for the next job change.

Although most employees are satisfied with the content work, they would like to have a well-defined and "powerful" designation. Explain the designations properly, especially to new people who just started or who will be working in the flat organization.

Work Content

When the Indian IT industry started, the scope of work executed in India was very limited. People perfected multiple skills so that they could easily shift from one project to another within or outside the company. They were the "jack of all trades," and eminently very "employable." However, after the Y2K (year 2000) passed, without the much-feared closing down of world systems, the scenario in India changed. During the depression of the early 2000's, many Indians returned home and product development companies started setting up their operations in India, while many service companies began taking more ownership in executing the client's project life cycle. All of these have led to a slow transformation of required skills—from seeking "jacks of all trades," to "masters of a few". This transformation of skills has lead to a dramatic change in the job landscape.

Domain Knowledge: This has started to become increasingly important. People have started choosing specific domains early in their career, wanting to develop significant expertise in it. Today, they are very well aware that while domain expertise would limit their options in a job change, the upside is that it will command them a higher salary and better technical challenges. Managers who were not required to possess significant technical expertise are now increasingly finding themselves to be knowledgeable in their domain.

Flexibility: Employees chosen for development, testing or any other function will find themselves slotted in the position for a long time, leading to extremely focused job experiences. So much so, that there are very specific roles like technical writing, quality assurance, product management, program management, technical marketing, system engineering, and so on. Software development alone contains, multiple phases, including design, code, debugging, unit testing, integration testing and many more. People are required to have different skills in different phases. A person that excels in all phases is very rare. This has triggered a need for sub-specialization. All these provide more avenues and additional people issues too. Job rotation becomes increasingly difficult, and managers need to be aware of how they encourage people to develop multiple skills over time. Managers in India today also have a formidable task to run the team with a mix of specialists and generalists in order to achieve the desired goal in a technology-intensive industry.

People Issues Viewed from Other Perspectives:

Self-induced

Most people issues fall under this category. Individuals are flooded with doubts, anxieties and misconceptions, leading to issues relegated to ignorance. One of the most common self-induced issues is an employee's belief that he or she is "being victimized". This occurs when an employee feels that their colleagues are preferred above him, or that he receives mundane tasks while managers assign others with challenging ones. These issues may also include appraisals, salary hikes, promotions, recognition and the list goes on.

The downward spiral of morale is quick and disastrous; the employee even rejects thoughts of embracing change, learning and adopting new skills, roles, and processes. Sometimes, even if the employee thinks that he or she has the skills to embrace change or can take up a challenge to move forward, he or she will still feel insecure. In a good organization, the leaders must ensure free access to advice and counsel that can help challenge individuals to evolve.

Induced by Management

Sometimes, managers are responsible for people issues. The management should explain and implement company policies for their employees. A company's leadership is also responsible in providing and setting the right expectations. It might happen that in spite of every care taken, people will still be dissatisfied. At this point, one can disagree and move forward. One key aspect people want to see is transparency, sincerity and honesty in reviewing issues. The true test of an organization in regards to handling people issues well is when people leave without any rancor and still rate their experience as having been "wonderful".

Induced by Peer

Peer pressure—if taken positively—can yield growth and superior results, while the downside can lead to teaming issues. Healthy peer pressure occurs when people learn from each other to set higher internal goals and succeed. Sometimes a high-performing peer might cause dissatisfaction among other team members. If a peer does not exude good social skills and does not mix well with the team, these issues are aggravated. The manager has to play a sensitive role in these cases. On one hand, the manager would want high-performing individuals to continue doing a great job, while on the other hand he also needs to maintain harmony within the team. There is no silver bullet for this problem. Sometimes, high performing employees can be given difficult and standalone tasks, so that their interaction within the team is limited, leading to less friction. A good management strategy is to ensure that a team has the right mix of skills. Despite best efforts, significant variations can continue in performance levels. Many a time, a management team makes the mistake of composing a team based solely on performance while discarding a teaming perspective. This will seldom guarantee success either for the individuals or the project.

Peer pressure can also arise from the work content. Some people succumb to thinking that the grass is greener the other side and that their peer's work content is better than their own. If the peer is on another team, this thought culminates in asking for a transfer to that team. While this could be a good possibility, how the manager decides and delivers his decision to the team member will make a big difference in allaying employee fears.

Induced by the Industry

Some people are very well aware that any good or bad industry news can affect them. The most commonly exchanged information is on salary hikes, designations, benefits and incentives. While this provides a good source of industry data and can help in revisiting policies, every company's policies are defined based on their needs and therefore they remain different—and this should be very apparent to each employee.

Working abroad or making a business trip is still a point of discussion, and part of career expectations. With more product ownership coming to companies in India, there may not be a business need to travel. Employees should understand this issue. The leaders will need to discuss this expectation early on and reinforce it from time to time.

People Management Summarized:

As a manager it is important to have utmost care and provide proper attention to the greatest assets i.e. people by developing and cultivating a good working relationship in the right environment which can encourage exchange of crisp and candid feedback for the desired result.

People Management Case Studies:

Case 6.1: As a Senior Director, you shift from the US office on a two-year assignment. Here you find that managers and directors in your team are not technically sound and do not participate in in-depth technical discussions. They spend most of their time in project management, risk analysis, communication to the US office and people management. You feel that if the India team is to take more ownership in defining and driving products in future, their technical content needs to increase, especially in the management level. You try to work with managers and directors to make sure that they understand the design and architecture properly to be able to ask the right questions. The team expands and triggers the creation of a new manager position. You promote one of your key technical representatives to a manager position based on desire expressed in an appraisal dialog. This also helps your purpose to augment technical depth within the management team.

You are happy that you have started a transformation in the company, but the contentment does not last long. In your quarterly skip-level meeting, one of the engineers under the new manager makes the following announcement:

"When you moved me from another manager's team to this new group, I was excited that I would be working on new and complex features that involved cutting edge technology. While the scope of work and the ownership in taking up the new challenge is very satisfying, I am not getting full support from my manager. Although we all respect him for his technical genius, I feel there is a glass wall between him and us. For any issue that comes up, I have to think multiple times before I can approach him so I will not look stupid in front of him. Though he listens and solves my problems at the earliest, I do not get the feeling of "being taken care of", which I used to get from my previous boss. He might be more suitable as an architect. You should check with the other employees as they too could feel the same way".

This strikes you like a thunderbolt. You pacify the engineer in your own way, but this leads to more soul searching. While this was going on, the HR sends a 360-degree feedback report to you regarding your own performance. You are surprised to find the following quote.

"Sometime he appears like a task master, who is only interested in getting the things done and not on improving the soft skill of team members."

"We work like a family, and his highly professional approach on talking only work at times makes me feel that he does not appreciate my personal circumstances and never offers to accommodate it in a win-win way. To approach him on non-work related items is a no-no."

What will be your reaction?

Case 6.2: You are a senior manager of a team having multiple managers reporting to you. One of the managers is discussing a particular person's fall in performance made during the last few months. This person joined the team a year back and the first six months went well. He used to interact with all the people in his team. In order to complete his task, he is required to interact with team members of other manager's team too. Due to his high rating last year, he was given new challenges.

The employees regard their manager well and you have the utmost trust in his judgment.

The first complaint came from your manager some three months back. In the last three months, you have heard that he remains silent in meetings, does not take up any additional work or even accomplish new work in his ownership area. As time progresses, the issue of him honoring his working hours becomes far more complicated (forget about stretching or working late). Although he delivers work assigned to him, he commits to fewer tasks. Only recently, the manager has asked you what actions should be taken.

At this time, you decided to get HR involved and the first advice you receive is to talk to the person (skip level). You did accompany the manager in talking with the engineer in the past, but it was a one-sided conversation and hence you agreed to this suggestion.

You setup a meeting with the person and receive the following statements:

"This is a complex project and there is no appreciation for my work, while other members who can speak and present well are being appreciated in the team meetings."

"My module has undergone so much requirement changes that I do not get proper support from my manager in communicating important issues to the other team, which makes me look as though I am consistently appearing in the critical pathway."

"Over a period of time, I find myself being micro-managed. However, I agree that I started taking less workload and have become less active in meetings."

What do you think is the issue?

Case 6.3: One of the engineers has been working in the company for the last five years. He is an upright citizen and has earned respect during his early years in this company. For the last couple of years, he has received an average rating. His manager is someone who joined the company a year back and is doing a good job in leading the team.

He has quickly earned the respect of his team members because of his project management skills and support in helping his team members during difficult times.

The engineer walks into the manager's office and says the following:

"As you know, I have been in the company for the last five years and have consistently provided high quality outputs. Lately, I have started feeling that I am no longer required in this company. The reason is simple; it is due to the recently concluded appraisal. Although you rated me average, which I have no qualms with, it hurts that you have not given me my due promotion. The person promoted to the next level does not have the same number of years of experience and has joined the company much later than me. You can ask any person in the team and most of them will not understand the criteria used in promoting him. I talked about my promotion last year with my previous manager and he said that I would have to wait another year for consideration. I do not want to have an argumentative session, but it is also true that my salary hike is moderate and does not reflect my true performance. I had expressed to you both these issues in my first meeting with you when you joined and you told me that you would look into it at the time of my next appraisal. Since it seems to be the same story this year, I feel very disappointed and I wonder whether my loyalty is not being appreciated in this company."

If you are in the manager's place, what will you do?

7 Execution is Everything

Setting up an India office sees realization only when the company achieves its objectives—in higher customer retention by delivering products and services faster, in flawless perfection, and within competitive pricing. Success of execution finally determines the success of an India operation and hence it will not be an exaggeration to say, "Execution is everything." Once the right infrastructure is set up, the best team is hired, and the right culture and policies are in place it is impractical to assume that the execution would be automatic. Establishing a strong foundation is just the beginning. Flawless execution is the key to institution building.

An excellent book entitled "Execution, The discipline of getting things done",[12] written by Larry Bossidy and Ram Charan, states "To understand execution, you have to keep three key points in mind: Execution is a discipline and integral to strategy; Execution is the major job of the business leader; Execution must be a core element of an organization's culture."

---

12. Execution, The Discipline of Getting Things Done, Larry Bossidy & Ram Charan, Crown Business, 2002

One should be prepared to face a rollercoaster ride during the execution phase: plenty of surprises and challenges are sure to abound.

There are four fundamental soft skills, referred to as ASAP, required by the management team for execution. By applying ASAP skills, one can execute "as soon as possible" in alignment with the market needs.

Soft Skills Required

A: Ability to Make Quick Decisions

A management team in India will often face dilemmas in their unstated scope of ownership while having to make decisions. Questions like, "Are we empowered by the parent company to take a decision?", or "Will they trust our decision?", and "Will they ask us to roll back our decisions?" will cause leaders to pause a while. These dilemmas lead them to a simple solution—wait on the parent company for guidance and decision-making. The first opportunity to prove the parent company is lost.

It is extremely important to keep the parent company in the loop, but it is equally important to win the trust and confidence by starting to undertake decisions locally. It has been frequently heard from companies in the U.S. that they opened up an India office only to find the entity quickly turn into a puppet team, whereas their earnest desire is that the India team stand up on its own. The more one delays in taking command, the more damage there will be in institution building.

Spending a lot of time to make a decision is a big hurdle in efficiency. Waiting to assimilate every bit of information is futile. While some decisions need to be revisited, it normally is not because they were arrived at hastily, but because there are new data or time has provided answers that might be contrary to the earlier decisions. Mistakes should teach lessons, but not hamper the speed of decision-making. If one has to revisit or reexamine less than 10% of decisions, the decision making process is good.

A parent company can help significantly in providing an outsider's views by weighing the pros and cons. They should welcome a team making independent decisions who continually keep them in the loop. This should allow the parent company to present them with more complex tasks, because they are confident in the information flow and in the way, the India company has maintained high transparency in resolving issues.

When the new management team starts showing their hold on the execution process and decision-making, the parent company starts relying increasingly on its capabilities and gets involved only in regards to critical issues.

S: Self Confidence

This does not require much elaboration. Self-confidence will enable fast decision making–and past experiences help in adding to this self-confidence. Self-confidence is especially required when there is a lack of consensus and decision-making is a major task. Self-confidence helps in rectifying issues and resolving dissonance amicably. Rarely will one see a new challenge identical to the previous one. For this reason, self-confidence can help the team conquer one challenge after another.

This skill alone is not sufficient. Self-confidence without any tangible results is a hollow claim. But, self-confidence can help in bringing early trust and dependency of the parent company towards the management team.

A: Always Think About What Can Go Wrong

This is important in making sure that the execution process will not stop, slow down or become irrelevant due to unforeseen issues. Andrew S. Grove in his book, "Only the Paranoid Survive,"[13] discusses strategic inflection points. In this case, it might be a tactical inflection point because the canvas might not be that large. One has to make many tactical decisions by keeping the strategic direction in mind. Not only does one have to think about potential issues, but one also needs

---

13. Only The Paranoid Survive, Andrew S. Grove, Harper Collins Business, 1988

to prepare the company, in case the issue becomes real. It is best to have an alternate plan or plans that will kick in, if the issue becomes reality.

Some key issues:

Human Resources

If a person leaves the company, is there a plan in place for someone to take on those responsibilities without losing time? Is there a primary and secondary ownership in place to take care of attrition? Is proper documentation and review of work available for new comers to begin execution without plenty of downtime?

Do we have a right mix of senior, middle and junior levels of professional in order to achieve high quality output? Is the team overly optimistic or pessimistic in committing a date?

Are we lowering the bar while hiring rapidly? Do we have a good training program in place so that senior people can spend less time in bringing people up to speed?

Does the India operation have sufficient management bandwidth? Are we training some of the managers? Are we preparing a few others? Do we need fresh blood from outside the management team to take us up to new heights? Do we have two ladders, so that technical folks do not clutter the management ladder due to a lack of technical ladder?

Will a new company policy de-motivate and demoralize a large section of employees? Will it be a salvageable situation or is there a wider ranging impact? How do we handle both scenarios?

What will happen to the existing team if there is a significant delay in decision making in the parent company regarding a new project? What will happen to people in case of shelving a particular product line or project?

How will we retain people who have specific or unique skills that are in demand in the industry?

What background checks are in place to avoid any person seeking employment on falsely produced data?

Technical Areas

Is the design modular and will it stand the test of time? Do we execute a prototype to ensure a validated design? Can the design scale for future requirements?

Is it better to build everything or can we plug in third party solutions for faster turnaround? Are the proper third-party tools preferred to help in development and testing? Does their roadmap backup ours? What type of support can we get from them? Do we need full source codes or just binaries?

Do they understand the requirement document well? Will India deliver the right content against the requirements? What type of reviews should be in place to avoid surprises?

Is software designed to take care of international language support in future? Can it run on various platforms in the future?

IT Infrastructure

Are proper backup policies in place? Is a disaster recovery plan in place? What will happen if there is disruption in the connectivity to the outside world? What alternatives or backup plans are there for the connectivity? How do we control or recover from a virus spread quickly?

Does the India office comply with the Information Technology act of the Government of India? How are we going to manage an IT crime? Is the India IT policy in alignment with the parent company policy?

Facility

Have we done safety checks of the building? Are the legal documents (hire or purchase) proper and is there no violation of the building sub-laws? Is there a proper provision for a fire escape? Do the employees practice a fire drill?

If the company is running transportation for the employees, what will happen if the vehicle meets with an accident? What will happen if that vehicle is responsible for the loss of life?

What measures are in place if an untoward situation occurs in the city? What measures are in place to avoid any theft? What steps should be taken in case this happens?

If the company runs a canteen facility, what are the company's responsibilities in case of negligent catering?

Others

Is the company in compliance with the Government regulation on Income Tax, Sales Tax, Company law, labor law, customs and STPI or EOU? Are government papers submitted on time?

Have proper steps been taken to avoid sexual discrimination and harassment at the work place? Does the company deposit the provident fund on time?

P: Patiently Impatient

Infectious impatience is key and is best to be followed the majority of the time. It allows people to feel that management is responsive and keen on walking the talk. It instills a sense of urgency and provides a feeling that their issues are resolved immediately—freeing them from unnecessary worries that happen when waiting for the issue's resolution. This saves hours, and in turns saves staff-days. As a result, it can pull in the schedule, develop internal buffers for unseen errors, or use newly allotted time for improving quality further. Time saved is time gained.

Testing the ASAP skills continuously throughout the execution process is important. During this stage, one might experience changes in team dynamics, fluctuating morale, wavering motivation, new technical and management challenges coming in periodically, miscommunication, major or minor changes in plan, change in organization structure and so on.

Equipped with ASAP skills, one can execute professionally by applying the following principles as the situation desires:

Hire the Best and it is Better to be Understaffed

Most of the malice in an organization occurs from overstaffing. While other factors could also influence issues, overstaffing is a major cause of work politics, favoritism, lay-offs, de-motivation, low morale, and so on.

Everyone joins an organization to do good work. Although people complain about having a lot of work, they complain even more when there is a lack of it. Idle minds wander and one of the first devils peek into peer's work, only to start "comparing and contrasting" work. This leads to de-motivation and a sense that the company is not fair towards all employees.

Companies in the U.S. are frequently under the misconception that hiring in India is a quick and rapid process. While hiring can be fast, quality hiring requires a good amount of time. When the hiring plan is not firm and yet the hiring continues at full speed, it might lead to quick overstaffing.

Understaffing can also lead to its own set of problems. The first of them is about delaying product development. This in turn leads to cutting down the scope of the India office's work and finally into hiring more at the headquarters or elsewhere. These are calls that the product management and senior management must take based on competition, prioritization of features, and time-to-market. The India operation should do its best in hiring, but should not fall into the trap of lowering the bar in recruitment under any circumstances, simply to meet the numbers.

Transparency and "Need to Know" Information Flow

Thirst for more information is natural. When the organization is small, everyone receives almost all information about the company, but as it starts becoming large, distribution of information begins on a need-to-know basis. This process should not be sudden but must ensure that employees can adjust to the changing environment. Sometimes, information will come with some lag. When this happens, the management needs to prepare the team for this transformation and do their best to ensure that work will not suffer due to the lack proper information. Nevertheless, it is important to make the big picture clear to the India team, so that they can make right decisions in their respective areas. Customer feedback should flow freely to the India operation, allowing them to keep improving the product.

It is very important to have a smooth flow of information among the multiple offices in different time zones, who are working together for a particular execution. Audio and video conference calls are required for this purpose. Having conference calls at odd hours is a discomfort to both U.S. and India operations, but both parties have to live with it. In order to be fair to the different geographies, odd-hour conference calls should be balanced to prevent any party from facing odd-hour calls for months or years.

Clear, Honest and Timely Communication

Communication is the key to success. Effective communication involves communicating with clear statements, wherein the other end also understands the statements clearly. Open-ended communication normally leads to misunderstanding and chaos. It is better to close the loop within a committed timeframe. "I will see" or "I will look into it" or "I see your point and let me think" are statements that do not have any closing timeline.

Communication is even more important in the case of hiring. Bringing a new recruit on board is easy, but keeping the employee happy and motivated requires a bigger effort. For example, an engineer hired may want to know whether he can transfer to another team, soon after joining. For this situation, the answer should be simple: The Company interviewed and hired him for a particular position based on his skills. For this reason, a transfer is not a possibility. There should not be any promise of consideration in the future. Company policy will dictate future transfers.

The communication cost in India has reduced significantly in the last 5-6 years and it will reduce further. People today rely heavily on email for communication. Compared to one phone call to a same or different geographical location that helps in resolving an issue immediately, closing an issue via email can start a chain of email that takes multiple days to close. This is also because people want to have a written record of all discussions on a topic. This works during normal times, but when the issue requires faster closure, emails might not be an appropriate medium. There will be some hesitations in calling people at different time zones at bizarre hours—painful yes, but very quick and helpful.

Beauty Lies in the Details

The ownership of products or projects in India is increasing and with this development, the expectation of the management team's technical knowledge increases as well. Gone are the days when the engineering management in India could be successful just by tracking a schedule, following a development processes and collecting a quality matrix. In order to be successful today, management must have the knack to ask the right technical questions and to gauge the severity of an issue. It is important for first level managers to be involved in detailed discussions, in addition to their management activities. The second level of management should also have a clear vision of the high-level design and architecture. This will enable the team to make right calls and present the right picture to the parent company.

Flexibility With Commitment

The productivity of the employee increases if he is free to choose his own working style, as long as he is aware of the delivery timeline and the quality of the output expected from him. For example, people can sometimes work from home provided they can publish the expected output during that time. This reduces the pressure on the manager to micromanage and they can spend productive time elsewhere. Employees will feel more responsible and accountable. This is applicable only for those people who have spent a number of years in the industry and are mature enough to plan their activities well.

Human resource policies serve as a framework, so that the team can adhere to general guidelines, but retain their flexibility based on their own circumstances. This is also the case in a large organization, where different projects or product lines can choose their own flexibilities.

The organization should be careful and understand that most time flexibilities start with very noble intentions and slowly become misused.

Product Belongs to the Company

People develop a sense of pride in their work, but can become too possessive at times. Some even go a step further and become emotional. It is important that the people feel proud of their work, but they should also understand that the product belongs to all who work for the company.

Every organization requires a dedicated team of people who give their best, but one needs to make sure that people have to rotate handling different jobs and roles within the company based on business needs. Job rotation will also help during attrition.

There are some murmurings, objections and questioning to this approach. People have various issues:

Will this affect my job security?

Is there a lack of trust from management?

How is my appraisal being done? Will I be penalized for others' mistakes?

Is the management worried about attrition?

Why should I own other's areas and be responsible for it?

Answer all questions upfront and respond to them immediately, removing doubts in people's minds.

The other issue can be at the management level. Sometimes, managers become possessive of their team and resist any transfer of resources from one team to another. They will volunteer their team members' help, but would insist on members returning to their team, or will lend members only so that the other manager can manage the technical issues of the project, while they retain control of their team. One needs to have a good discussion with the managers to understand these concerns and find a win-win solution. The workplace is dynamic and the manager who is at the receiving end today understands that tomorrow might be his or her turn.

Matrix management is an aspect that needs serious consideration. By default, managers tend to follow the linear line of reporting, thereby leading to miscommunication or not providing timely communication to other stakeholders. In addition, the staff (those who do not have anyone reporting to them) can sometimes become more vulnerable to the issue. This will hinder their contribution, as they need to get their ideas conveyed through discussions and negotiations rather than through direct hierarchy. It adds up to an additional responsibility on the second and higher level management in India to ensure that the product or project should be executed smoothly, keeping all the stakeholders informed and ensuring that nothing falls through the cracks. The most important aspect is to provide the right information to the right people at the right time.

Adhering to the Development Process

Every organization has a defined development process. They may have certified (ISO or CMM or some other) development processes or may be in the process of certifying them. Some might have a strong internal process and may not want to go for certification. The development process provides an opportunity for the whole team to speak the same language and understand milestones in the same way. This will also help in providing clear guidelines and expectations of various teams at different phases. Some managers feel this is an overhead or an obstacle from achieving results on time, or simply a tool for his manager to judge his performance. It is best to train managers and engineers to master the proper usage of tools and techniques of the process to get the desired benefit.

Requirement & Design Phase:

This phase requires a good amount of time investment from both the parent and Indian operations. It is better to conduct extensive face-to-face discussions during this phase. In addition, clearly written documents are important to avoid any ambiguity. Due to the geographical issues of working, the teams cannot discuss the project in a room or draw on whiteboards to show changes in the flow of execution. A team of any size cannot travel and stay indefinitely at any location.

Realize that the India team might not be exposed to customer requirements or the deployed scenario and therefore some of the requirements might not be understood in the same way that the customer-facing team understands them. The negotiations for the feature will be from a schedule perspective and not from the customer perspective, in which case the parent company needs to prioritize a list that can help the team in India. It will also help if the parent company reviews the architecture and other documents written by the India team based on requirements discussions, to ensure that they understood the project correctly.

Change Request and its Impact on Various Functional Areas:

Change request is a part of life and although prevalent at the initial stages, it can come at any time during the execution cycle. It is normal to expect the accommodation of change request in the same schedule. However, to the India team, it appears to be a dictum to accommodate it in the existing schedule itself, but the management team struggles to fit it in. Clear and direct communication about the risks associated in accommodating the change request in the schedule is required.

Sometimes managers in the parent company go one-step further and try to juggle the resource and activities for the India team on their own. The management team in India perceives this as a sign of mistrust. On the other hand, by empowering the local manager and providing him guidance on prioritization, the results will be far more satisfying.

Handover Criteria Between Various Phases:

Define the handover criteria in every project very clearly. Whether it is a document, code, report, quality matrix, or a combination of all, it must be stated clearly. This is not only required for a cross-geography handover, but also when handing over to another team within the same geography. Highlight issues like exceptions in the execution, risk in the status and weak areas wherein the other team should spend more time. These are normally hidden somewhere in the detailed report and will take time to be discovered and acted upon. The teams should be encouraged to report the bad news first before the good news. When informed of the bad news, it is important to focus on the issue and not on the person delivering the news.

Escalation of Issues:

Escalating an issue at the right time is a skill requiring fine mastery. A premature escalation of an issue leads to the belief that the team has not done enough groundwork. If escalated late, it will lead to the belief that the team either was hiding the bad news or did not understand the seriousness of it in time, leading to a point where its ability to be rectified is impossible. A simple solution to this lies in periodic status reports, which track and monitor every serious issue across the geography, ensuring the proper time for escalation.

Availability of the Third-Party Deliverables in Meeting the Schedule:

Although the normal tendency is to build everything internally, it is good to evaluate third party products and services that can help in expediting the development process and help in meeting the market needs.

In the end, it is good to involve the India team in the evaluation process of third party products or services.

As far as product evaluation is concerned, keep the following points in mind:

Usage: Will this be part of the resulting product? Will this be used for testing the product or will this be used for compatibility testing with the product?

License: Is this a development license or runtime license? Floating or fixed? International or India specific?

Warranty & Support that will suit a company's requirement:

Vendor selection: Based on the company's guideline, one should proceed with the vendor selection. It would be better if you have an option to identify the vendor who can provide good support and share the roadmap (in case your product is critically dependent on their roadmap) and can be flexible in accommodating your request.

As far as outsourcing work is concerned, the parent companies normally manage the outsource partner in India directly from headquarters, but it is also true that sometimes they ask the Indian offshore centers to manage the outsource partner from the India office. The advantages of managing from India are many: Easy to have periodic face-to-face project review. Any demo or prototype can be arranged and the periodic progress can be visibly monitored. The company also saves on travel budget.

The India operation can also decide to outsource some of its work either by having onsite contractors or by providing a piece of project to a local service company. The decision to go for outsourcing by an India offshore center is based on the same parameters by the parent company as discussed in Chapter 3.

It is important to manage outsource partners well. The management team of India offshore center needs to decide whether the project requires onsite contractors or offsite contractors. If the outsourced work is somewhat self-contained, the interfaces are well defined and the team size required will be medium to high, then it is better to go for offsite outsourcing by putting proper checks and balances in place (i.e. follow proper project management practices and reviews). The management team needs to have good communication skills to integrate offsite teams into one big team to achieve the desired goal. There is no additional effort required in managing onsite contractors provided both organizations maintain transparency in discussing issues related to or influencing the onsite contractors frequently.

Making Sure the Infrastructure is Ready for a Particular Phase:

There will need to be a lead-time in sending equipment from the U.S. to India, so that it becomes available in India when required. Similarly, local purchases in India have different lead times for different hardware and software. These lead-times should be an aspect included in the schedule. If the approval is required from the parent company, then they need to ensure that it comes within the timeline required. For some of the third party software, the support in India may take longer compared to the parent company. During critical phases, the parent company should step in to provide help by interacting with these companies.

Teaming:

The mantra of "collectively we can win" provides the recipe for success and acts as a powerful unifying force in keeping teams together. To achieve success, the company should have extraordinary teamwork across various sub-teams. In order to help the teamwork process, managers should have a goal in their appraisal aimed at helping other managers meet their goal. In such an instance, they will make attendance compulsory for their senior folks in the cross-functional review, cross-functional issue resolution and resource sharing. This will help in quickly changing the priority of the engineer at any critical time.

No product development can ever succeed if done in silos. All teams must be kept in the loop and this requires a strong program manager or a release manager. Excellent coordination and communication skills are required to make this position successful.

Quality Bound vs. Time-Bound Release:

This is a decision that every management faces regularly. The India execution team normally does not have full visibility into customer dynamics, quarterly revenue targets, market intelligence and competitive advantages. Therefore, they normally follow an engineering release schedule. For them, the commitment to keep this date is paramount.

The management team in the parent company has to play a very active role to establish the quality of the product when nearing the release. They should ask specific questions, go through the quality data together with the India management team and jointly work out the risk items and resolution plans. This will help in ascertaining the realistic schedule to decide on the release date. The interpretation and understanding of the quality data should be uniform across locations (and it should be good to follow the same quality matrix).

The Indian management team should state assumptions clearly. Sometimes, verbal communications and emails of the past may not have conveyed the seriousness of the issue. It may also be unable to get the right attention at the parent company. To avoid this, mention issues regularly in the status report together with the severity to ascertain the risk in the release.

Expectation from the Parent Company

To build an excellent execution team in India that the global organization appreciates, the stakeholders must be brought up to speed in regards to execution and moves up the value chain. The following four mantras can help in laying the foundation.

The first and foremost mantra is to be one-step ahead of the parent company. Simply put, try not to be a bottleneck in the execution. Many discussions at the corporate offices happen on various plans, changing priorities and other driving factors based on customer inputs and financial considerations. This juggling and re-juggling is continuous in any growing and dynamic company—not limited to just the senior management, but also within the execution staff. If the India team keeps itself one-step ahead of the parent company, it will earn respect, appreciation and in turn more ownership in the challenging projects.

The second mantra is not to do just what is asked, but to suggest better ways of doing things. It can be anything from providing alternative solutions of merits and demerits or taking initiative in driving technological advancements. This would include comprehensive analysis of the data rather than just a supplier of data, suggestions on good tools for debugging and testing or best practices that can make a process simpler and better. Any knowledge of good off-the-shelf products and suggestions in reducing the cycle time are all welcome signals.

The third mantra is to suggest some ways of solving the problem, rather than merely stating the problem. Giving a couple of ways to resolve the issue demonstrates that the team in India has put in careful thought. This will make life easier for the parent company and they can reach a mutual decision with India team sooner.

The last mantra is to think beyond India. The India team should volunteer to resolve issues at other international locations or help in seeding team at new locations. Sending some people for a short time and/or doing part of the project in India (which is important for the customer and the required skill set is available) is critical in the path to mitigating risk. This will provide visibility at a global level.

Miscellaneous

Various geo-political and legal issues might influence product development. One needs to be careful in the product development if the product displays the map of the world. A few countries are in dispute on some of the territories and hence there might be objections from those countries, especially if you are planning to sell the product in that country. Sometimes, the country of the parent organization bans some of the high-end technologies e.g. encryption algorithms, nuclear technologies or some innovative technologies when exported and used in other countries. It does not matter whether the company has a branch office in those countries or not, they will not be allowed to develop or use the technology and product. The Intellectual Property rules and regulations are different in different countries and it is important to know and adhere to these rules. If any open source code is used as a part of the product, then the copyright and other legal aspects should be taken care of. This is also applicable to any third party licenses used at different geographical locations.

To end this section, let us also look at the following aspects, which play a major role in execution.

Seating Arrangement to Make Execution Successful

Facility planning can help in making the execution successful. The scope of this section is limited to the facility in the same city. Sometimes, one gets the space in the same building or in an adjacent building. It might also be at a different location in the same city.

Let us Take Two scenarios:

1. The success of the development team is to provide high quality deliverables to the test team by reducing bugs. The success of the test team is to prevent the customer from finding any bugs. In one organization there is a big space, the lab is in the center. The smaller section of the lab is for development, which has entryway for the development team, and the other one is the test lab that has entry for the test team from the other side. Both teams cannot see each other due to the lab between them. The interactions are limited to emails and the meetings. Somehow, a culture was set-up to have a jubilation roar when the test team found a critical issue and the intensity increases as one approaches the release date. The development team easily hears the jubilation, causing bitterness within the group. Slowly, the relationship reaches a level where the acrimonious exchanges occur through email or in meeting rooms. They start becoming two warring tribes, which makes the job of the CCB (Change Control Board) more difficult.

2. There is a plan to form a new team for the new product line. There is no single large space available and therefore they have to split the team into two adjacent buildings. With this set up, half of the

team served development in one building and the other half the test team in another building. The development team has to look over any critical issue raised by the test team. The person has to come from another building to look into the issue. Sometimes, they take a couple of hours and finally appear with tea and sandwich in hand. The test person is in a dilemma. He has to wait to show the bug; otherwise development might want him to reproduce the issue, making success in getting the issue reproduced a remote possibility. Waiting for the developer is affecting his own schedule. Near the release cycle, when the critical and difficult bugs are coming up, this scenario becomes more frequent. The test person becomes irritable, and decides to collect the log, send it to development for analysis and move on to additional tests. He has stopped thinking about the overall product quality because he starts worrying about the schedule alone.

There are many factors in teaming, but it is best to analyze it from a facility perspective. In the first case, it would be wise to have one big lab without any physical partition between the test and the development areas. Earmark the spaces separately for development and test, so that they can track their own inventories. They should have the lab established on one side, so that test and development can sit together to facilitate human interaction. Interaction will help in developing professional bonding, which can lead to the discussion of issues more freely. Some people feel that development and test sitting together might affect independent thinking. Performing proper development processes will prevent this issue from happening.

In the second case, it would have been better that the division should have happened based on the interaction level. It is true that there will be some impact on teamwork when one separates the seating due to floor or building or location, but as much as possible, teams that require a high degree of interaction should sit together. Therefore, the split in the second case could yield better result if done based on functional level interaction.

It is important that the layout of the floor should propel the growth of the relationship building to enhance the teaming. It is better to take a larger space on one floor, and make sure that the full execution team can sit together. This is applicable if the execution team's size is small, but sometimes a large project might require a team size of over 300. In that case, it is important to apply due diligence. Teamwork is not only required between development and test, but also with system engineering, quality, technical writers and support team.

Another important topic of discussion is regarding cubicles. The height of the cubicle should be around four feet four inches; so that if a person is standing in their cubicle, they can make eye contact with the person in the other cubicle. This will encourage cross-cubicle communication. Once you increase the height of the cubicle to five feet or so, the teaming reduces drastically because team members cannot engage in cross-cubicle communication. On one hand, it provides a sense of privacy to the engineer, but it also provides a pathway to isolation. Any quick discussion or quick input required or a quick call for the meeting, will take more time in these types of setups. In some organizations wherein teams work well with low cubicle heights, they experience a sudden reduction in teaming once moved to the new location where the cubicle height was high.

Although large organizations have global standards of defining the work area that need to be followed, if the India management team has the flexibility of defining its own, it should apply a lower height cubicle.

Execution is Everything Summarized:

Execution is a very big challenge faced by all offshore centers. Flawless execution will take the center to new heights. Proper execution will allow for the attainment of more responsibility, an increase in motivated team members and a free flow of respect from the parent company. On the other hand if not done properly the center will take much more time to move up the value chain or could even remain stagnate for years. The management teams equipped with ASAP skills, should foster an environment of trust and open communication across geographies where people can freely exchange good and bad news, new ideas and initiative, without having any fear of repercussion which will instill the feeling of one large successful team. This environment of "Twin brothers (parent and offshore)" is important for the success of the organization as it will avoid silos which tend to appear due to location constraints.

Execution is Everything Case Studies:

Case 7.1: A large US-based multinational company has many sectors. One of the sectors is "communication and networking". They have a team in India that works together with the team in the US. They have a main product line where the Indian team plays a critical role in contributing to every release. Annually, one major and one minor release take place. These products have a huge install base across the globe. In addition to this main line product, the sector also has one network-monitoring platform sold to the customer and used by the customer to check real time health of the network, develop real time report or generate data for post processing. The release cycle of the main line product bundles this platform because most of the features in the main line product needs the support from this particular platform. The management wants to start a new product line for a different market segment and wants to free up resources in the US for this purpose. Therefore, they decide to shift the entire platform development and release to India. The Indian management has asked you to take up the leadership role for this. You have agreed to perform one minor release with the US and guarantee that you can be on your own during the next major release. You have got some good resources shifted from another team and you hired some new people. You divide the whole team into two, headed by a development manager and test manager and they both report to you. You form a core technical team, which you send to the US for transition.

The India team receives proper support and guidance from the US team and the minor release go well. Slowly, the US team takes up a new project. Planning of the new major release is complete and India receives the list of features and major milestones. You and your team go through the requirements and the release date and conclude that you cannot deliver it on time with all the features requested in this release. You face a dilemma for your next step.

Case 7.2 One large Multinational company based in the US is working on a few key technology areas. The product management wants to add a new interface to this revenue-generating product that will open up a new market segment in East Europe, South Asia and Africa. The management asked Alex to get it done from one of the development centers in these geographies. He has heard good stories from his colleagues in getting the job done from India. He decides to visit India to explore the opportunity. The India development center has asked Shyam, who has worked closely with Alex's peer in other projects, to prepare the material for discussion with Alex during his visit. If both parties agree to the project, then Shyam has to get this one executed.

Alex presents the slides and states the following:

1. Marketing has yet to define a clear and crisp requirement
2. I have no staff to work on this project except one person, who could elaborate the interface and provide any help in getting it integrated in the overall product.
3. I would like to hear the risks upfront and the support you expect from me, as I hate surprises later on.
4. Sticking to schedule and ensuring high quality is essential.

Shyam lists out the following:

1. The schedule will be dependent upon getting the clear requirement by a certain date.
2. Decision on buying a third party solution for this interface or to build one, requires a consensus between the two teams, with India driving the process.
3. The team will also require help in reviewing the intermediate milestone and deliverables.
4. He also elaborated the frequency and plan of status reporting and escalation of the issue.

Alex and Shyam agree to start the project.

Alex thinks he has to spend time only on weekly conference calls and to provide necessary help as and when they ask for it. He can concentrate on other high priority items and it is good that India has taken over the full ownership.

Shyam is delighted that he has taken the full ownership of a project that is starting from scratch. This well-contained project does not have many stakeholders. Hence, it will reduce the communication overhead.

The project starts.

The third party stack evaluation is complete and Shyam sends the slides with the pros and cons of various third party solutions together with the effort in developing it from scratch. He recommends one of the third party solutions that require minimum customization.

Alex is happy with the progress.

The first shock comes to Shyam, when the marketing team drops one of the major features for which he had chosen for the solution, and adds a new one. Shyam raises this issue with Alex. The other surprise comes when the customization effort that he initially estimated increased multi-fold after receiving the detailed feature description. Shyam again raises the issue to Alex. Alex still wants to ensure Shyam that the schedule can be met. Shyam requests his manager to help him in getting more resources and he gets it.

Alex worries and tries to convince the marketing team to de-prioritize a few sub-features, as they cannot develop it within the schedule. The Marketing team de-prioritizes it, but by then the release time is approaching fast and Shyam has little confidence to deliver the toned down list on time and with quality. He sends the first release to Alex's team, which lands up with multiple issues, including third party licensing. It was fire fighting on a daily basis causing de-motivation and burn-out in the team.

Case 7.3 Revenue figures from one of the divisions of a US company are not looking good. This division is the main driver in showing loss for the overall company in four quarters in a row. The CEO has asked the VP of that particular engineering division to reduce the cost. He further suggests cutting down the product portfolios by declaring an end-of-life for those products, which are at loss, but advises him to check the customers' contracts clearly.

This puts the VP in a dilemma, as most of his loss-making products were profitable until last year. In addition, the company launched the product recently with the obligation of three-years of support. He blames sales for not doing a good job, as he feels that the competitor's product is worse than his company's product. His job is to reduce costs. He consults his management team and decides to shift testing activity on one of the products to India. Depending on the success, they might also consider shifting the development activities of the same product.

The Test Director in the US agrees to shift test activities to India. The US team will perform the last phase of testing, which requires complete checking of the product before the release to customer. He advises the Director in India to come to the US with a few key people and develop a plan for the transition. The word spreads like a jungle fire and people working on that project become jittery about their future. People start to look for lateral shifts to other divisions. Key performers accommodate in other divisions, while few others receive outside jobs. Some others continue to stay but keep looking for other outside sources.

By the time the India team gears up to visit the US and starts working on the transition, they find only a few people remaining in the team. On inspection, they find some of the documents not up to date, some information old, and getting correct information from people hits a roadblock due to key personnel not working with the company any more, while some accepted relocation to another department and not being able to recall procedure completely. During the whole process, a tense environment prevails, causing sentiments on both sides.

The US team that would continue to stay for the last phase of testing is suspicious whether the new team can perform with the same coordination and understanding. The Development team worries how the process of bug raising and fixing will work due to time difference, but the more important issue in the back of their mind is if the same thing could happen to them.

Under all this chaos, the Indian team has to do reverse engineering by going through test cases and test scripts etc. to figure out the test plan. They start forming the team and recruiting new resources. They start the tests and the difficult issues take long periods to fix as the development team needs to have more logs and they are unable to use the system to analyze what has gone wrong. There is also a lack of understanding due to the discrepancies in the document vis-à-vis actual implementation, causing the team to overthrow a few test cases and write it afresh. This causes missed commitment and slippage in schedule. This difficult period makes a few people in India jittery and they start quitting their job. The issue escalates to management at both locations, where it actually reflects upon sentiment and hurts feelings rather than addressing the issue.

8 Conclusion

The first reaction to the question of opening up an India office is of surprise, and disbelief that this global phenomenon is going to happen here too. Once this message has settled in, a feeling of confusion will appear on how to make it happen. The headache has just started.

A good upfront and realistic plan, which lays a roadmap for the India operation, can be the starting point. This plan must be revisited and revised frequently based on new information, change in direction and new expectations. The leader should be passionate and of high caliber. They should be prepared to involve themselves personally in every stage of building the operation. The management team should think about building a powerful brand to help in recruitment and have a great work culture which can motivate people (even in the worst of times) to ensure the success of the operation.

The understanding of cultural differences should always help in foreseeing the issue. The Management team should walk the talk that will help in setting the right culture in the organization. The policies should be set by keeping local practices in mind and by aligning with the policies of the parent company as much as possible.

Trust building among the operations based in different geographies is key to ensuring smooth execution and a feeling that "together we can win", as opposed to individual paths ruining cohesiveness, which can only hinder success.

Most issues in regards to building an Indian operation can be prevented by applying the lessons learnt in this book. If any issue becomes a reality, these lessons can serve as a guide to the path of resolution. A new age has been entered, where the globalization of companies is no longer a luxury, but a necessity. With the vast wealth of knowledge and competence that lay within India, an opening of an India operation and running it successfully, no longer needs to be a recipe for disaster, but instead a blueprint for success.

A Terms and Terminology

One can open the India Offshore Center using four different schemes. Each one has its own entry criteria and provides different benefits. One needs to choose carefully. These schemes are

- STP (Software Technology Parks)

- EHTP (Electronics Hardware Technology Parks)

- EOU (Export Oriented Unit)

- SEZ (Special Economic Zone)

Under any of the schemes, one will encounter some of the terms below, during the formation of the company and later in running the operation. These are just brief explanations and it is best to take proper advice from legal or tax firms in order to make sure that they are sound. Government policies are constantly amended, so it is best to keep up with the latest guidelines.

Transfer Pricing: This states that an international transaction should occur at "arm's length". There are various methods mentioned in the act, which can help in achieving said transaction, such as:

- Comparable uncontrolled price method

- Resale price method

- Cost plus method

- Profit split method

- Transaction net margin method

The "Cost plus method" is by far the most popular. This refers to the total cost in running the operation added to a percentage of cost used in determining the billing for the parent company. The transfer pricing study, which external tax agencies usually conduct, determines the exact percentage. For example, if the study shows x%, then the invoice amount will be 1.x times the total cost. This will lead to an accumulation of money in India. The company can then use this money to purchase assets in India or they can choose to send it back to the parent company by paying applicable taxes in India.

Permanent Establishment: Legally, offshore center is a separate entity. However, according to Indian law, any person holding a foreign passport and on the parent company payroll that stays in India for a continuous period or has accumulated enough days in that financial year, is permitted to have a permanent establishment of the parent company in India. This should be very carefully considered with legal and tax advisors.

Paid up capital refers to capital the parent company can invest in setting up the center. The company can choose to start with lower capital while continuing to add more as it grows. Beyond a certain amount, one has to keep a full time company secretary as per law.

Advance Against Future Billing: In the initial period, offshore center will not be able to generate enough revenue to sustain itself. This is more acute in the case of growing organizations. In this case, offshore center can take money from the parent company and get this adjusted against the future billing, but one needs to complete this within the stipulated period defined by the government.

Second-Hand Assets: For the new entity, there is a regulation that governs what will be the maximum percentage of capital goods, which can be under the "used" goods category.

Capital Limit: One needs to take prior permission from the Government on the total value of imports that offshore center is planning to get in. If they foresee a need to bump up that figure, they need to do so. No import is possible above the approved limit.

Labor Law on Number of Employees: One needs to take specific permission from the Government whether the number of employees will be less than 25, less than 49, less than 99, or more. One can start with a lower number but the number can be increased.

Provident Fund (PF): This is like the 401K program in the US. The company can have this implemented once they reach 20 employees, which would include contractors. It is beneficial to have contractors working in offshore center, which are already under the PF scheme of their own companies. In that case, the figure of 20 employees will not consider contractors. Beyond a certain period of uninterrupted service, a contractor can claim a job legally; however, this rarely happens.

Late Working for Female Employees: This is a state government regulation and it differs from state to state.

ESOP (Employee Stock Options Plan): The Government of India recognizes the ESOP of the parent company as extended to the employees of an Indian subsidiary. They are recognized as "qualified" if registered within six months of issuing the first grant to the Indian employees.

Patent Filing: It is better to understand the laws clearly. Currently, if any Indian resident is filing the patent for the parent company and decides not to file the same in India, then he or she needs proper approval from the Indian Government, before filing the patent overseas.

There has to be a "compliance calendar", i.e. a calendar that should clearly state the last dates of filing various government reports on a monthly, quarterly and yearly basis. It is important to file these reports on time. It is equally important to keep an eye on ever-changing government regulations from time to time.

B List of Vendors

Vendor management takes a lot of time. A sample list of vendors is mentioned below. This is not an exhaustive list but provides an overview of the complexities involved.

- Legal firm

- Auditor firm

- Tax filing firm (it can be a separate team in the same company such as an Auditor, but a new interface to manage)

- Internal Auditor company

- Accounting firm: As per Government regulations, an accounting firm should be different from the auditors and internal auditors

- Payroll firm (if separate from accounting) to take care of the payroll and labor law related filings

- Direct interaction with STPI/EOU/EHTP/SEZ on some issues

- Indirect interaction with STPI/EOU/EHTP/SEZ, VAT, Sales Tax etc. through a firm that can do return filings for them.

- Builder or landlord, if the office is on lease/rental

- Building maintenance, if different from landlord

- Bank for company accounts

- Custom clearance Agency for shipments

- Office security agency: sometimes security can also manage the front office.

- Office maintenance company (it can be same with a security agency or it can be a different)

- A System maintenance firm can take care of all IT needs, if outsourced

Though the vendors do provide very good services, one has to go through every report carefully in order to ensure that the report is per expectations. This is due to various factors: The growth in Indian economy provides more business opportunities to vendor firms, and therefore focus on details will be abridged. These firms experience attrition and one may have to continuously deal with new hires. They will often come in briefed on the history and relationship; but in order to get the desired result, one should be prepared to spend time in providing the correct perspective and the recent history.

C Policies to Address

Salary Structure

Salary structure is prone to changes in the Personal income tax rules, which are amended once a year as per India Government budget. It is advisable to follow the simple and safe approach on salary structure, as some of the tax benefits that the Government provides can sometimes lead to different interpretations, creating new unforeseen issues.

Gift Policies

Clearly state the gift policy in the company especially when dealing with any external agencies. There are some festivals in India where it is a ritual to exchange gifts in business dealings. It should be appropriate to document the limits under which one can receive and give gifts. It is appropriate to mention the type of gifts that can be given or received. Normally flowers, sweets, cookies, dry fruit, and things of this nature are acceptable. If someone has received any gift, which is beyond the approved limit, or have received a gift, which is deemed unacceptable, then the committee should reject it or declare its proper usage or disposal.

Leave Policies

Labor laws dictate the different types of leaves available to employees. This serves as a framework in implementing policies. The exact number of leave options will vary among companies and data from various companies can be used in order to frame one's own policy. Normally, one selects a number that is similar to the parent company's leave policies. It is important to observe mandatory national holidays and state holidays. In addition, one has to provide additional holidays. There are restricted holidays too, which means that the person can choose holidays from a list supplied by the government.

Travel Policies

This is a sensitive topic and one should be clear when formulating this policy. One should have a clear and written policy for domestic and international travel. If required, one can divide the domestic policy based on the classification of cities; similarly, one can divide the international policy based on countries. These policies should consider multiple factors.

Domestic Travel Should Mention:

- Air or Train travel and the type of class

- Per diem allowance or fully reimbursed on actual

    - If the stay is long, sometimes a mix is also allowed

    - Expenses for client entertainment are normally reimbursed

    - The allowance may differ according to the type of cities based on the cost of living

- Sometimes the accommodation etc. are already negotiated at the corporate level

International:

- Air travel together with the type of class

    - Sometimes the class is dependent upon the distance of travel

- Per diem or reimbursement based on receipts

  - Sometimes it can be a mix of both, where boarding and transportation can be reimbursed on an per diem basis

- For long term stay

  - Clarity on spouse and/or dependent children tickets

  - Clarity on whether or not a ticket in order to visit home for self and/or family will be provided

An employee should declare any money saved during domestic or international travel to the company for income tax purposes.

IT Policies

The Government of India has come out with the Information Technology Act 2000. The IT policy of the company must abide by this in addition to the overall corporate policy. As far as using the internet is concerned, various companies have different policies. Some limit the usage to a few hours and some make it available all the time. Some deactivate it permanently and some deactivate only chat and email access. Some provide this facility only in their library or in other common locations.

Other Policies

Normally, different companies have different policies in regards to the probation period. A probation period is a training period. Some policies are specific only to a probation period. At the end of the probation period, the person will become a full-fledged employee.

In India, the payroll cycle is executed on a monthly basis. However, the notice period (advance notice required in case of resignation) can differ from company to company, but it often ranges from one to three months.

As far as sexual discrimination and harassment are concerned, a company needs to follow specific laws. In India, a special committee needs to be in place to address these issues. There are strict labor laws in case of a layoff or firing. A good approach is to provide feedback to the person. It is also best to provide them with a timeline to find another suitable job. Companies can define their own policy on non-solicitation and confidentiality.

D Solutions to Case Studies

Case Solution Pointers: Chapter 2: Choosing the Right Leader

Case 2.1:

If you are looking for too many skill sets in one person, then you should prioritize them.

It is often difficult to find an exact match. One needs to compromise on some skills and complement then make up for lacking skills by hiring management and/or technical positions.

It does not hurt to take a risk. If an individual does not come close to the expectations that have been set, a termination of the relationship is possible.

Are you extremely passionate in setting the center and finding the right leader? Alternatively, are you being forced to take this up? Are you doing your best?

In addition, you might want to consider these things.

Do you have a convincing story?

Do you address every concern a person may have?

Are you looking for a specific attitude and a potential to develop skills while an individual is on the job?

Are you prepared to give him or her more salary if you find the candidate suitable?

Are you looking to be a micro-manager?

Are you involving senior people in the parent company to talk with the candidates to reassure them about company prospects?

Talk with parent company to find trade-off criteria e.g. Time line, provide someone to fill in temporarily, and re-scope the position (higher or lower).

Go back to the ones you had interviewed earlier – either they may be free now or they may know someone interested.

Case 2.2:

The family issue e.g. spouse might not have found a suitable job or may have encountered some health issues in regards to their children. Alternatively, it may be the children, who have yet to adjust to their new surroundings.

The odd hour conference calls and frequent travels to the parent company have caused burnout.

The company may have not given considerations about income tax implications initially and now it might be affecting them negatively because it may not have an attractive relocation package.

These could also be the reasons...

It takes time to adjust when an initial outpour of relatives initially excites, although later on it could become overbearing.

The spouse was not fully convinced of the shift. She keeps finding faults at the slightest opportunity and thus, troubles continue to compound.

He might not be getting proper support from the parent company in closing issues quickly.

The scope and expansion plan of India might have been re-structured, which might have de-motivated him.

It looks to be far too late in the game for this one; the person should be keeping much closer contact with the parent company.

Instead of pondering too many questions, ask the people directly about the real motivation for wanting to go. By identifying the core issue, one can spend time and effort in resolving the real issues. Be careful not to spend too much time in speculation.

Case 2.3:

You will define the organization structure clearly and ensure that people follow it. They must know their expectations and you need to make sure expectations are met.

You might setup a mailing list that includes the three of you. By doing so, you can discuss and resolve the issues among key people easily.

You can tell them that their success is intertwined and hence they need to work together.

You can have one separate and one joint "weekly call", so that there are no hidden feelings.

Discuss issues among the three of you, including complaints against each other. This helps in arriving at a common understanding quickly and avoids possible negative impacts.

You should ensure that team members do not exploit the situation, which can be detrimental to the company?

You might have to fly down and sort out the issue.

In addition, what you can also do is...

Encourage the practice of appreciating employees and asking them to appreciate their peers.

Tell them to help each other in one's absence or consult each other in resolving issues from any of their areas. This will encourage bonding.

Discuss any people issues in the team among the three of you, so that a common message can be sent to the employees.

Case Solution Pointers: Chapter 3: Setting up the Operations

Case 3.1:

You should assemble all stakeholders in one call and prioritize the list.

You can review the list and decide which can be outsourced and which requires in-house execution.

You can also decide on the activities you can do on your own and ones that require help from the parent company.

You can also think of...

Communication is the key in any setting – whether for employees, US stakeholders, vendors and outsourcers.

Avoid any temporary solution, as it will haunt you in future.

Most of the time vendors are overloaded with multiple assignments. In order to get the desired result one needs to insert incentives and penalty clauses in the contract.

You need to setup a timeline based action plan and drive it to closure by seeking all possible help from stakeholders.

You need to have a running list of open items, which should be updated frequently and reviewed with stakeholders.

Case 3.2:

He should know his desires and preferences in choosing one of the options or he can ask for more time

If he receives an opinion from a vendor on any of the issues in the support function and if he is not sure of its accuracy then he should verify this by asking the other vendor. This information can then be used to provide proper suggestions to the parent company.

He should seek clarity in role and responsibility in matrix management. He should develop his skill in working in matrix management e.g. flow of information and decision-making

He should improve his communication skill and make frequent voice contact with Finance and HR in the US.

Case Solution Pointers: Chapter 4: Recruitment Challenges

Case 4.1:

You can put a half page advertisement on the front page of a prominent newspaper.

You can sign up with multiple recruiters to get better results, but make sure that similar resumes from different recruiters are handled carefully.

You can identify a few educational institutions and give presentations to spread awareness.

You can contact key candidates and convince them about the organization.You can think of opening a HR position to handle this, if not present or increase the strength in HR.

Also:

Checking out similar companies in the local industry and looking for news about a division or company that is folding. These instances can give you the benefit of hiring a full team.

Have you hired a PR agency that can help you in brand building? Have you done few press releases and positioned your company well in the job market?

Set up job fairs and seminars, and then invite a popular public figure known in India, who is in the board or management team in the parent company.

Have you utilized some of the university alumni mailing list?

Have you utilized all major job portals?

It might be somewhat easy once you hire the core team as referrals from existing employees and job portals can help in hiring more.

Be prompt in all correspondence, written or verbal.

Case 4.2:

You should not compromise on the quality of the candidate and pay them higher (at least to the core team) otherwise, you will not be able to deliver.

Any market cannot sustain this growth in salary and hence it should stabilize in future, and therefore it is fine to proceed with increased budget now.

Other issues to think about:

Do I have to pay more to attract and form my core team?

For senior employees the ratio of 1:4 will be more skewed, as for junior employees it should be fine. Have you taken a salary survey report from a reliable source by targeting similar types of companies and then positioning it appropriately?

The average cost of the operation will even-out once as the hiring continues to bring aboard individuals with varied experience levels and profiles.

If the type of work does not warrant utilizing the offshore center then outsourcing can be a good option. This can be done directly from the US office or can be done from an India offshore center as well. Please read Chapter 3.

Case 4.3:

You can ask the VP or senior director to address these people.

You can ask the VP to setup a new timeline for the parallel release so that you can provide a clear message to potential hires.

You can negotiate for ownership of a few features in India once you complete this existing release and if a parallel release team is not in future plans.

In addition, you can think about:

Without any clear deliverables or a clear timeline, it is difficult to retain people. People cannot continue to read documents for long hours.

The message, which the initial team takes back to India, is the key for motivating the newly formed team.

It might be best if a few senior technical people, from the U.S., shift to India for a couple of months to work with the team (after they have returned from the US) to make sure that India team can deliver new features. This will also send a message that team in India is capable and can take more ownership in future.

Less experienced people might be more wiling to travel and stay for longer periods at the parent company but more experienced people are not as willing, and hence sending them for longer periods might not work.

You can ask for transfer of few people from other divisions in India to form a critical mass for your project.

You can also motivate people (particularly senior ones) by involving them in decisions such as recruitment, scoping out of work, evaluating any third party software, etc. This will keep them meaningfully occupied and they will feel that they are learning new things.

Case 4.4:

Start having one on one dialog with each engineer.

Provide a presentation to people on product roadmap and market strategy.

Ask HR to work out a plan that can motivate people, for example retention-bonuses.

You can also think about...

Asking the senior management of engineering and marketing to come to India provide a full roadmap that can reassure people on work challenges

You can also ask for more ownership in the product if possible.

You can also ask to add more functions (based on the corporate plan) to the India office to motivate people as they can feel that the operation is growing.

You can work of skill improvement for key engineers e.g. provide some direct customer experience, if they do not have it.

Case Solution Pointers: Chapter 5: Cultures & Policies

Case 5.1:

One should provide regular feedback of the work and provide suggestions of improvement not only on the technical side, but also on soft skills. At the time of appraisal, one should provide feedback through examples.

Can HR help in explaining this hike?

Junior folks will discuss these details amongst themselves and hence one should plan to explain the action and respond accordingly.

You should also think about...

Is the work clearly differentiated, even if it is in the same project?

Did the promotion policy communicate clearly? Were the skills needed for improvement before the promotion clearly communicated to engineers?

Should HR help in explaining why some get less of a hike in spite of getting a better rating?

Manager should update Supervisor on:

- Give examples of Compare & Contrast Culture.

- Situation with Engineer #3 and #1.

Supervisor can do the following:

- The Manager requires much more coaching.

- Together with manager, they can role-play and perform what-if situations.

- Put together a script of responses.

- Very important to have expectations set and examples of how the engineers can improve their ranking.

Case 5.2:

Pacify both parties individually.

Provide feedback to them based on what you have heard about them. Each one needs to look at the others perspective and understand the difficulties faced.

Ask her to have a periodic conference call with you so that she can escalate issues to you.

Also:

Arrange a meeting with both of them in order to provide open discussion.

Write down the rules of engagement and the process of communication.

It might be helpful to setup daily calls between the two of them for the next few weeks in order to build a trusting and open relationship amongst them.

Case Solution Pointers: Chapter 6: People Management

Case 6.1

Did I do something wrong in transferring a technical person to management, even if this is was what he wanted?

We are in a product development environment irrespective of geography, there is a difference between each countries director and managerial skill sets.

In India, people expect more from their managers.

In the US, we need to be sensitive about getting too personal, but in India, it appears to be a different ball game.

More:

Effective people management provides less time for technical details and hence restricting managers/directors to focus only on risk resolutions.

Is it that a comparatively young workplace requires more attention and hence people management is more time consuming?

Why is it that this new manager who was technically sound, has now chosen the management ladder? Is the technical ladder strong and attractive enough to lure technical people towards it, without cluttering the management ladder? If one treats symptoms, then problems are only temporarily pacified.

Is the management tag (i.e. being a manager and not a pure techie) more socially acceptable in India?

No manager can be a perfect mix of technical and people skills, but an effort should be made by the senior manager to complement the skills lacking in the subordinate so that employees are not impacted.

Case 6.2:

Is it high-pressure work or some interpersonal issue?

Is there any across team issue? If so then why he is not seeking support from his manager?

Is it high handedness by the manager?

Is he de-motivated due to salary or promotion?

Is he undergoing a crisis in his personal life?

Can the issue be resolved by job rotation or by setting up an adequate goal for the engineer or by having frequent skip level meetings until the issue is settled?

Or a mix of multiple issues or maybe it is something more.

Case 6.3:

Has the previous manager promised him or just informed him of the policy on promotion.

Any future commitment should be based on business requirements.

To discuss with HR and to revisit his overall compensation and see if there is any mistake so that a proper response can be made.

The promotion criteria should be explained well.

Also:

Have you provided honest and direct feedback on skills required for the next level? How did he measure up against those skills?

If he meets the above criteria, will you really promote him or is there a fixed number or ratio that is used? If so, will HR make an exception?

Is he causing discontent within the team or has he taken it maturely?

Do you want to do a one on one comparison with the other engineers, or do you want to deal with the case separately and avoid having to compare?

Also, what if the individual decides to leave? What impact will it have on team spirit and on deliverables? What actions does one need to take into consideration to minimize the impact?

Case Solutions Pointers: Chapter 7: Execution is Everything

Case 7.1:

To communicate clearly to the manager in India and in the US

Ask your manager in India to shift some senior people from other project to work on this for sometime. Alternatively, you can ask for help from a contractor for a short period.

Have you provided various options to the management i.e. feature prioritization, fixing of old issues, phased release, additional resources or outsourcing few activities?

Also:

Is this a one-time issue?

Have you thought about what went wrong? Did you clearly ask for the design documents from the Manager in US who was responsible for it? If it is not available, have you asked them to develop one? When doing the reverse engineering did you use the proper resources? Did your team go through most of the code and understand it?

Did you encourage escalation of issues even though escalation might not be taken in a positive way?

You should ask probing questions to gauge another person's understanding and confidence on the subject.

Ultimately believing through experience and witnessing that bearers of bad news are not shot, but even encouraged and rewarded.

Did you apply soft skill "Always think what can go wrong" together with the principles like "beauty lies in details" and "escalation of issues"?

If it happens again, one might have to see how one can involve themselves into the planning process when the feature discussion is taking place. This can be done by requesting U.S. managers to assign one person to this job or asking them to receive an individual from India for that particular role and stationing them in the U.S.

Case 7.2:

Is the communication between Alex and Shyam candid?

Did Alex and Shyam look inside the company to find a similar solution before proceeding to buy a third party solution?

Faster development leads to less flexibility in requirement changes and/or requirement creep. Is it communicated well by Alex and Shyam.

Why is the contract not properly scanned for copyright, licensing and other details?

You might plan on asking a few probing questions to get to the root cause and solution:

1. Was there access to Alex's status reports, so that Shyam could have full visibility on the complete product line?
2. Shyam's manager should have been proactive in asking probing questions and finding potential issues, as Shyam could have been focused on day-to-day activities.
3. Is one identified person from Alex's side sufficient or do they need a few more?
4. Is a third party solution decision a hasty one? Was it evaluated without prototyping? Was the product management team involved in the decision making of the third party solution?
5. Did Shyam escalate the situation properly?
6. Did Alex utilize senior management in influencing or convincing the product management on feature sets?

7. When the project was reset, did Alex do sufficient research and understand the full impact of dropping one feature and adding another feature? Did Alex successfully escalate this?

8. Did Shyam follow "clear, honest and timely communication" to get the right attention on his issues at appropriate time? or was it Alex who thought that all these issues should be handled by India independently and he just needed to provide pointers? Is the handshake properly defined and agreed?

Case 7.3:

There is no silver bullet to answer this. Sometimes, one has to go through a tedious and long process, while identifying intermediate milestones for confidence building and learn lessons to improve the process.

Are the project scope, team formation and timeline communicated well from the beginning for both the team?

Were the key stakeholders involved in the transition plan since the beginning? Are they committed to making it happen?

Are people issues addressed adequately at both the sites? Moreover, have they been sharing the plan for the future clearly?

What is the strategy of the Indian team for the transition?

You Might be Planning to ask a Few Probing Questions to Come to the Root Cause and Solution:

Did they put some intermediate milestones in order to build confidence and to learn lessons that may improve the process?

Are managers having frequent one on one interactions to understand people issues and act accordingly? A few people in the US could be retained for some more time, not only for the transition, but also until a release is made in India.

Another cultural item here is that people tend to think one can only get a good appraisal by working on the most sought after project. Managers need to reinforce their employees that they need to shift from project to project occasionally. It may be recognized that the person is ready to help the team and that teamwork and flexibility are highly valued by the management.

Why is the shift system not introduced in India (to provide some overlap with the development team in the US and to increase efficiency)?

Did a clear message go out to the development team, which states that the end goal is to make the product profitable and that they should do their best to make this model work?

One needs to work on four pronged strategy of understanding and delivering the test responsibility, understanding the features together with development and identifying a champion who can support in issue resolution, build a similar champion with US test team who can do last phase testing, and not procrastinate on any issue and to tackle it at the earliest.

Success ties everyone together, and interpersonal issues will reduce significantly only by having a good relationship, which can happen by frequent visits by all levels.

Large problems can be avoided by dealing with issues early having open communications and clear expectations set up front.

About the Author

Utkarsh Rai, head of India Operations, Infinera, started his career in the late eighties as one of the first few batches of IT professionals who joined Siemens in India and went on to work in Siemens Germany for a stint. The team returned to form a spin-off called Siemens Information Systems in India, an IT company.

Utkarsh moved on to work with Adaptec in Silicon Valley, where he was involved in a full-blown product development lifecycle. In the boom period of the late nineties, when Indians flooded the U.S. in search of IT jobs, he could see India—and Bangalore, specifically—being a center for product development. He flew against the winds of the time and joined the Global Software Group at Motorola in Bangalore.

This opportunity provided him with the experience in leading large teams, recruiting a large pool of engineers and handling complex people issues. When the first Motorola facility in Bangalore were filling up, the team was asked to move to a new location in Bangalore, which provided him an additional opportunity to learn about the challenges of starting fresh. As he grew to become a member of the senior management team of Motorola in Bangalore, he addressed operational issues like crisis management, setting up the right compensation and benefits, adherence to government regulations and execution challenges.

This experience prepared him for his current role as the head of India operations for Infinera—a startup in digital optical networking—a position that he took in early 2003. At that time, there were few people on board, and he was responsible for reinforcing the company culture and its policies, ramping up the team in number and in skills, and over the past four years, he has achieved a smooth execution with ownership and drive from India. He understands the Indian Government's regulations and operational compliance, and setup a new facility in line with the expansion plan. The single largest success has been in managing and developing the greatest asset–people.

Infinera went IPO in June 2007.

All these experiences triggered Utkarsh to write a book on India operations, which he sees as a great way to share his knowledge and experience with wider audience. Utkarsh can be reached at utkarshrai@yahoo.com

Create Thought Leadership for your Company

Books deliver instant credibility to the author. Having an MBA or PhD is great, however, putting the word "author" in front of your name is similar to using the letters PHD or MBA. You are no long Michael Green, you are "Author Michael Green."

Books give you a platform to stand on. They help you to:

- Demonstrate your thought leadership
- Generate leads

Books deliver increased revenue, particularly indirect revenue

- A typical consultant will make 3x in indirect revenue for every dollar they make on book sales

Books are better than a business card. They are:

- More powerful than white papers
- An item that makes it to the book shelf vs. the circular file
- The best tschocke you can give at a conference

Why wait to write your book?

Check out other companies that have built credibility by writing and publishing a book through Happy About

Contact Happy About at 408-257-3000 or go to http://happyabout.info.

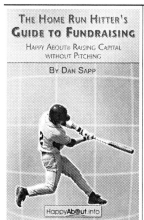

LaVergne, TN USA
29 December 2010
210462LV00004B/43/A